D0204361

BULLYPROOF YOUR CHILD
FOR LIFE

BULLYPROOF
Your Child for Life

Protect Your Child
from **Teasing**, **Taunting**,
and **Bullying**
for Good

JOEL HABER, PH.D.
"The Bully Coach"

with **JENNA GLATZER**

A PERIGEE BOOK

A PERIGEE BOOK
Published by the Penguin Group
Penguin Group (USA) Inc.
375 Hudson Street, New York, New York 10014, USA
Penguin Group (Canada), 90 Eglinton Avenue East, Suite 700, Toronto, Ontario M4P 2Y3, Canada
(a division of Pearson Penguin Canada Inc.) • Penguin Books Ltd., 80 Strand, London WC2R 0RL,
England • Penguin Group Ireland, 25 St. Stephen's Green, Dublin 2, Ireland (a division of Penguin Books
Ltd.) • Penguin Group (Australia), 250 Camberwell Road, Camberwell, Victoria 3124, Australia
(a division of Pearson Australia Group Pty. Ltd.) • Penguin Books India Pvt. Ltd., 11 Community Centre,
Panchsheel Park, New Delhi—110 017, India • Penguin Group (NZ), 67 Apollo Drive, Rosedale, North
Shore 0745, Auckland, New Zealand (a division of Pearson New Zealand Ltd.) • Penguin Books (South
Africa) (Pty.) Ltd., 24 Sturdee Avenue, Rosebank, Johannesburg 2196, South Africa

Penguin Books Ltd., Registered Offices: 80 Strand, London WC2R 0RL, England

While the author has made every effort to provide accurate telephone numbers and Internet addresses at
the time of publication, neither the publisher nor the author assumes any responsibility for errors, or for
changes that occur after publication. Further, the publisher does not have any control over and does not
assume any responsibility for author or third-party websites or their content.

Copyright © 2007 by Joel Haber, Ph.D.
Cover art by Superstock
Cover design by Liz Sheehan
Text design by Kristin del Rosario

All rights reserved.
No part of this book may be reproduced, scanned, or distributed in any printed or electronic form without
permission. Please do not participate in or encourage piracy of copyrighted materials in violation of the
author's rights. Purchase only authorized editions.
PERIGEE is a registered trademark of Penguin Group (USA) Inc.
The "P" design is a trademark belonging to Penguin Group (USA) Inc.

First edition: August 2007

Library of Congress Cataloging-in-Publication Data

Haber, Joel David, 1957–
    Bullyproof your child for life : protect your child from teasing, taunting, and bullying for good / Joel
Haber with Jenna Glatzer.— 1st ed.
        p. cm.
    Includes bibliographical references and index.
    ISBN-13: 978-0-399-53318-1 (alk. paper)
    1. Bullying. 2. Bullying—Prevention. 3. Child psychology. 4. Parenting. I. Glatzer, Jenna.
II. Title.
    BF637.B85H313 2007
    649.6'4—dc22   2007011496

PRINTED IN THE UNITED STATES OF AMERICA

10   9   8   7   6   5   4   3

PUBLISHER'S NOTE: Neither the publisher nor the author is engaged in rendering professional advice or
services to the individual reader. The ideas, procedures, and suggestions contained in this book are not
intended as a substitute for consulting with your physician or licensed health service provider. All matters
regarding your health require medical supervision. Neither the author nor the publisher shall be liable or
responsible for any loss or damage allegedly arising from any information or suggestion in this book.

Most Perigee books are available at special quantity discounts for bulk purchases for sales promotions,
premiums, fund-raising, or educational use. Special books, or book excerpts, can also be created to fit
specific needs. For details, write: Special Markets, Penguin Group (USA) Inc., 375 Hudson Street, New
York, New York 10014.

This book is dedicated to all those kids and adults who have faced a challenge like bullying and found ways to overcome the heartaches. It's not the problem that one faces in life, it's how you make it through that defines who you are. I've always been taught to keep at something until you get it right, and I hope those who face bullying issues can find the strength to do just that. This is also dedicated to my father, Wilfred, whose guidance and direction are ever present.

ACKNOWLEDGMENTS

There is no one more important to thank than my family, who had to deal with more than my share of time away from them to work on material and information for this book. My wife, Cindy, provided constant encouragement, support, evenness, and editorial guidance to bring this project to fruition. My son, Scott, had a perspective on today's youth that I sought out and valued. My daughter, Alyssa, had fabulous insight and understanding about kids and tweens that always made me smile.

Can anyone really thank a mother enough for continued belief and support of her son? If I could, my mother, Evelyn, would receive the kudos. My in-laws, Rocky and Seymour, sent me everything they found to read about bullying and I thank them. Thanks to my sister, Staci, for always encouraging me to reach for more.

My choice in a coauthor could not have been more on the mark. Jenna Glatzer is a fabulous person and writer. She was able to take volumes of material, discussions, and information and synthesize it into words that made this process feel easy when compared to my first book. Her experiences and passion about this topic, her talent and style made me enjoy this work so much more than I already do. Although I knew Jenna was the right one to partner with from the beginning, my respect and admiration for her continue to grow.

My literary agent, Barrett Neville, is a gem in his own right. I certainly felt blessed by his encouragement, directness, honesty, writing skill, and trusting quality, which was a fabulous combination of traits. His guidance gave me the encouragement to take my work on bullying to a new level by publishing this book with Penguin/Perigee.

My editor, Marian Lizzi at Perigee, deserves much gratitude for her dedication to this book, and her interest and willingness to pursue this and bring it to publication with generosity and vision.

My most valuable source of expert advice is the countless kids, clients, parents, and educators who have been a privilege to work beside in the last twenty years. This book is dedicated to all those who have been touched by bullying problems. I get up every day thanking my lucky stars that I can give a little back to all those people who have touched me with their stories, hurts, and successes. If I am able to help even one person with this book, then I feel successful.

I want to thank the American Camp Association for having the confidence in me to bring my knowledge and expertise to the "camp world." In this regard, I want to express gratitude to those camps that bring me back year after year to train their staff and improve the emotional and physical safety of their camp families. Peter Landman of Camp Kennybrook has been my biggest supporter, and I thank him for bringing me into this wonderful organization. There are countless other directors and staff who know how important they have been to me, and I thank them all.

Thanks to all the educators and parents who bring me to speak to their organizations and encourage me to share my "pearls" to improve their communication and skills. Thanks to psychologist Ellen Medd at the Wampus School for her consistent and continued support and friendship.

Thanks to Suzanne Reiffel and Erica Ross, who help keep me smiling week to week and give me so much collegial support. I look forward to the Tool Kits for Kids era.

Lastly, my friends are such a huge part of my life and always inspire me. I would need a book just to thank you all completely, but I hope you know how valuable you are. I don't know how often I've shown you along the way how much I appreciate you and how much I have appreciated your continued questions: "How's the book coming along? Did you see this today on the news? Check out this . . ." It all has meant so much and thank you!

CONTENTS

INTRODUCTION

Just about everyone has a bullying story. Mine happened when I was eleven years old. Every day after school, children of all ages played on my block on Long Island, New York. The house we grew up in was close to the next house and it was up to me to make my own good time with whoever was out to play that day. Some days were more relaxed and easygoing because of the makeup of the group of kids, but there were two kids who could ruin the mood and tone of the whole group just by their presence. It was as if a storm cloud would come overhead and break the silence with lightning and thunder without warning. All the other kids felt scared and tense, wondering if the lightning would strike them that day.

I was a little short for my age, not aggressive by nature, and tried to avoid conflict. Billy, on the other hand, was a pretty big kid, fifteen years old, popular, affable, and aggressive. He loved to make other kids laugh by torturing one of us with others looking on. John, who tailed him, was my age, fun to play with, but really mean whenever Billy, the teen I would now label "the big bully," was around. I never quite understood what made John turn mean whenever Billy was around, but I could feel my stomach sink when the two of them were outside together.

There was a period of time when John would tease, taunt, and physically knock me off the fence across the street whenever I wasn't paying attention to him. He would always walk over to Billy after an attack and look to him to receive that victorious "high five." All this happened when Billy was there, and I tried to stay out of the way of both of them whenever I could. This became very difficult and I would come home pretty miserable and dejected for what seemed to be an eternity.

Running home to my room, I would try to bypass my family— but I wasn't too successful at this because the back steps to my room were through the kitchen and living room. This meant meeting one of my parents along the way. I remember my mother feeling upset about these incidents, and trying to reassure me that it would stop as I grew and got older. I remember my father coming home late and hearing about these incidents. He felt so angry about my helplessness, and I in turn experienced his anger as something to fear.

In the meantime, I remember thinking food would comfort me, staring into the refrigerator endlessly, never knowing what I really wanted. I remember turning my anger and rage on my sister, who was three years younger than I was. It seemed like we were always fighting, and in hindsight, it felt pretty good to take out my frustration on her because she was an easy target for me.

My father talked to me about sticking up for myself, and came up with a plan to teach me to defend myself. Unless I learned how to fight back with my fists, he thought, I was going to be teased forever. I remember how driven he was to teach me the ropes. He never knew that I thought to myself, "I'll never hit another kid." I never told him that, but just tried to convey to him that this idea wasn't going to work by rolling my eyes and kind of going along with the plan.

One day he arrived home with a punching bag. It took two days to put up the bag in the garage. He presented it to me proudly . . . and I couldn't reach it. I just stared at it above me. I remember my mother shaking her head, and how I felt a sense of reprieve for the moment of truth. My father ended up spending hours lowering it to a height I could use, while I hoped this idea would pass very quickly.

My first instructions were awkward. I missed the bag, couldn't get a cadence, felt frustrated, but I didn't feel that I could quit and disappoint my father. Saying no to him was not in my vocabulary back then. There was a schedule to punch the bag each day, practicing different kinds of punches and moves to and from the bag. I would like to tell you I became proficient at this, but I didn't. However, I became adept enough to make my father believe I could handle myself outside if the boys bullied me again. Even though the plan was to have me stand up to John when threatened, I never quite thought that I would actually have to punch someone.

The day of reckoning came on a summer afternoon I'll never forget. I was outside playing, and Billy and John had started name-calling and getting aggressive with me. I was turning to go home (my usual tactic) when I noticed my father standing in the doorway of our house watching the situation intently. I hesitated, looked back at John, and experienced a moment of panic. I had nowhere to go. I can still feel the anxiety rush that came over me at that moment.

What would anyone do in that situation? When I ask my audiences what they think I did at that moment, the room is usually split between running away or standing there and hitting this boy to avoid the pain of my father's disappointment. I must have turned my head a hundred times before I turned around and hit John square in the mouth. Blood gushed from his mouth and he burst into tears. I ran home mortified that I had done this to him. (I've thought to this day that this experience contributed to my becoming a psychologist.)

People ask me whether I felt bullied by my father. My father's intention was to help me and not to hurt me, and this makes all the difference when thinking about bullying. Although my father was much more powerful in his influence over me, I never felt his intent was bad and, in fact, I knew it was just the opposite. He didn't bully me, because his intention was good. However, his power was scary to me, and I have always been fascinated by this power dynamic and the issues involved. Unequal power is one of the significant components of bullying, but it's not enough on its own. This book will begin by addressing the definitions and issues of bullying, and how the power dynamic becomes a critical piece in understanding bullying.

When I share this story, most people figure that this must have stopped the bullying. Regrettably, it did not, and actually made John more creative in ways to try to catch me off guard. I think it is important for parents to be aware of their own anger and belief that aggression toward another in retaliation will equal the score. Unfortunately, that kind of response may escalate the problem and make matters worse. Part of this book will address the kinds of responses that are appropriate and most helpful to parents when bullyproofing their children from these incidents.

In the early 1980s, I began my career as a psychologist working on violence prevention. I was trained as a researcher and clinician and published papers in graduate school. In my first year of a job directing a pain center in a medical school, I saw a patient with a complicated history: Sharon had a very unusual pain problem that seemed to defy biological explanation. The physicians asked me to evaluate her because she seemed quite comfortable discussing her pain and needing her seventh surgery in a three-year period for chronic intractable pain. They thought it was odd that she wasn't in the least bit distressed about needing more surgery, so they wanted me to interview her and figure out if there was something more going on.

She did ostensibly appear to be very comfortable with surgery, but I noticed a slight twitch when I casually asked about her marriage. After several interviews and support, it became clear that she was a woman who was severely abused at the hands of her husband, and would gain reprieve from the abuse with a medical condition that her husband could see. She found an adaptive coping response in cutting off circulation to her limbs at times to create pain and discomfort rather than face abuse. Inflicting pain on herself that created a visible medical condition to her husband was the only way she knew how to make him pity her enough to stop hurting her for a while.

I followed my instinct after this case and became involved in uncovering the roots of violence and power in these medical cases. My work and research led me to work with families with abuse— the abusers, the victims, and their children. The histories of these abusers were pretty clear. Children who went unchecked as bullies became abusive spouses. As the medical and mental health consultant on the New York State Governor's Commission on Domestic Violence, I became a trainer in the domestic violence field for several years and lectured about violence to medical and mental health professionals. I taught others about the effects of violence, power imbalances, and the cost of violence to the medical and mental health communities.

Many years later, after a presentation, a school principal approached me asking for help on the bullying problems being faced in the school. I met with a representative group of faculty, administration, and parents about their concerns. Together, we put together a plan to face the bullying issue in their school head-on. Although this project grew a hundred times more than I expected, I was struck by an enormous sense of pride in helping families and a school community begin to tackle this problem. I think back on that year as a labor of love and the beginning of my real work in the bullying field.

What better way to stop the pattern of violence in adults than to uncover the problem where it really starts? I realized this was my true calling. Ever since that time, I've been traveling to schools, summer camps, and sports programs to shed light on the bullying crisis and provide practical solutions. I speak to thousands of parents every year, and am the American Camp Association's official bullying consultant, so I've also spoken with thousands of camp counselors and directors.

And I solve their bullying problems.

Both in private practice and in these group settings, I work directly with all the people who affect the bullying dynamic—kids, parents, and the other adults in the kids' lives. I listen, come up with solutions, then we try them out and find out what works. The methods I'm going to teach you are tried and true and can be effective in any bullying situation for boys or girls from preschool to college.

My work has earned me the moniker "The Bully Coach" and appearances all over the media, including the *New York Times* and CBS News. At most of the presentations I've done, I've collected surveys to find out more about the scope of the bullying problem today, trends we need to be aware of, what works and what doesn't. And each time I speak, people ask me if I've written a book about bullying.

I have now. It's been my life's mission to prevent violence in all its forms—physical and emotional—and I hope this book will help spread the knowledge I've gained. Moreover, I hope it will help you personally to help your child.

In this book, I'll teach you my "Bullyproofing Prescription," a set of instructions for adults to use with kids to get them out of bullying situations and keep them out of bullying situations. These aren't goofy comeback lines, and we won't get into too much theoretical discussion about the bully's sad home life or the state of society. What you need are practical answers to help your child *right now*, and I will provide them.

You're going to learn how to get your child to open up to you; how to teach your child resilience; what the most important factor is in repelling bullies; how to approach a teacher, principal, coach, or camp director with your concerns; how to track a cyberbully; how to help without taking over; what to say when it seems no one's listening; and more. We'll do all this with sample scripts and exercises, written policies you can show to authority figures, and checklists to help you follow each step.

The bullying statistics are daunting; together, we can change them. I hope this is the last book on bullying you'll ever need.

ONE

Bullying Isn't Just a Playground Problem

For generations, we've heard and passed on the same advice about how to deal with bullies—and yet, the bullying problem seems to be getting worse, not better. Maybe that's because the advice doesn't work?

Ignore the bullies and they'll go away.

Bullying is a normal rite of passage.

Just tell the teacher and it'll stop.

The bully will stop picking on you if you learn how to fight.

These are the lines we've been fed—and maybe repeated ourselves. But the truth is that, as adults, we know deep down that some of these comments are absurd. What other kinds of problems are ever solved by ignoring them? What's normal about feeling abused?

When I was growing up, bullying was assumed to be a rite of passage. If you got beat up on the playground, that was supposed to toughen you up and show you how to "be a man." If kids called you names, that was "just teasing," and you were told to ignore it and it would stop. And almost no one talked about bullying among girls.

The good news is that society is taking bullying a lot more seriously these days. The bad news is that it took tragedies like school shootings to make us wake up.

Bullying is abuse, and it carries serious short-term and long-term consequences for all involved: the bullies, the targets, and the observers. Nearly everyone can remember that white-hot feeling when a bully said something meant to humiliate, or the time you tried to will yourself invisible so a clique wouldn't torment you in the locker room, even twenty or thirty years after it happened. Nearly everyone can remember the poor kid who was at the bottom of the social totem pole at school, and many of us can remember wishing to help, but keeping our mouths shut out of fear of being the next target or looking "uncool."

As adults, if someone harasses us, we don't have to deal with that person anymore. But children are legally obligated to share space with their harassers at school all day, every weekday. It's torment. And we owe it to these kids to help them feel safe, both physically and emotionally. Nothing is more important.

The clichés don't work. But I know the tools that *do* work, and by the time you finish reading this book, so will you. If you know a child who's hurting, we're going to get to the bottom of it and help fix it.

To do that, we're going to need to speak the same language. So let's go over the core concepts about bullying: what it is, who does it, what forms it takes, and the consequences.

What Is Bullying?

Bullying is a repeated and/or chronic pattern of hurtful behavior involving intent to maintain an imbalance of power. What this means is that a bully finds satisfaction in harming people whom he considers weaker to build up his own sense of power. It's important to differentiate bullying from fighting, the latter of which is really about an escalation of conflict and is normal. Kids roughhouse and may yell at each other or shove each other without a bullying element to it.

Bullying isn't about working out a conflict, and it isn't between evenly matched opponents. It crosses the line into unequal power dynamics where one person wants to control another. The bully believes the target is weaker in some way, whether that's physical, mental, social, emotional, or a combination. Bullies get satisfaction from harming their targets. If the behavior is left unchecked, it can intensify someone's (the bully's) power at the expense of someone else (the target).

Why Is It Getting Worse?

People sometimes ask me if there's a "bullying gene." No, not as far as we can tell. Is it because of neglectful parents, birth order, the media . . . ? Probably a little of everything you'd imagine.

Babies are born with certain temperaments. Some are passive. Others are tense, aggressive, or bubbly. You can tell early on if a child has a disposition that's prone to aggression—but that doesn't tell you if that child will become a bully. Nature is one part of the equation; nurture is the other.

The Madness of the Media

The media is a hotly controversial subject when it comes to violence and bullying. There are those who argue for opposing sides of the issue: either that the media creates violent kids, or that the media has nothing to do with creating violence. I believe that the truth falls a bit in between: The media makes it far worse for kids who already have aggressive tendencies.

Bullying has been normalized all over television. If you take a good look at reality programming, you'll notice how highly bullying behaviors are prized. There are actually shows where thousands of people volunteer to compete for a job with an abusive boss: FOX's short-lived *My Big, Fat Obnoxious Boss*, an apparent spoof on Donald Trump's *The Apprentice*, was a prank on the contestants. They thought they were competing for an executive job with a company called Iocor, when in fact the company didn't exist, and the boss was an actor. But they were put through degrading trials, inappropriate sexual remarks, unethical tasks, and verbal abuse in the hopes of landing this imaginary job—and we call this entertainment.

We also call it entertainment when Simon Cowell humiliates hapless contestants on *American Idol*, insulting them to the point of tears. Simon is rewarded for his verbal bullying with riches and fame. On *Growing Up Gotti*, young people watched and learned that the privileged boys can not only get away with awful behavior at others' expense, but they can be on the cover of magazines, praised as heartthrobs.

Even television *commercials* are getting worse and worse. While growing up, children are subjected to thousands of commercials with violent content.

Add to that violent video games, song lyrics, and music videos. All children are exposed to some violence in the media, even if parents do their best to monitor a child's activities. But not all kids internalize these messages the same way. Violent messages reinforce an already aggressive child's belief that fighting is a good way to gain power. They do not make good kids "turn bad."

Parenting Models

Are parents to "blame" when children are bullies or targets? Not always . . . but often, they have a lot to do with it.

Sometimes I see parents who tell me, "I don't know what happened. I have three great kids, and one who's a bully." It's pretty safe to assume that the parenting style is *not* largely to blame for the bully's behaviors in a situation like that, though the parents may inadvertently be rewarding or reinforcing the bullying behavior.

But in many cases, it's pretty easy to see where the child got the notion that bullying is okay. Bullying parents often rear bullying kids. And the way parents resolve conflicts between themselves creates a model for children—if one parent is usually "the winner" and the other is "the loser" in arguments, children can learn to identify with one or the other, thus becoming either the bully or the target.

In the next chapter, we'll explore this dynamic more closely, and examine how your behavior as a parent may encourage bullying or target behavior . . . even despite your best intentions.

New Bullying Technology: The Internet and Cell Phones

Along with new communication technology comes new opportunity for harassment. Some of the worst forms of bullying today are things you and I probably couldn't even have imagined in our youth.

Kids today are being threatened in anonymous e-mails and instant messages. Rumors are spread about them on websites that can be accessed by anyone across the globe with a modem. Embarrassing photos and diary excerpts are posted on message boards and forwarded among students.

They're receiving threats and harassment by text messages on their cell phones. They're participating in and victims of "three-ways," where one peer sets up another peer to say bad things about a third person—who is actually listening in, or reading the e-mails or instant messages.

New technology has made it easier for people who might otherwise be on the fence about it to become bullies. It also aids in the escalation of bullying. Anonymity demolishes much of the fear of retribution or consequences, and can even remove feelings of guilt or empathy—after all, the bully doesn't have to see the tears in the target's eyes when the humiliating words are received.

Who Are the Bullies?

Although most kids will "test out" bullying by testing out their power, the majority quickly discover they're not cut out for it. A child proves to be a true bully if he keeps up the role for months or years, loses his empathy with these incidents, or if his initial forays into bullying are exceptionally abusive.

Note that bullies are not typically jealous of the kids they pick on, and they don't usually have low self-esteem. That's another myth—one that experts believed for decades until psychological tests showed that bullies typically had self-esteem to spare.

When I was growing up, the stereotype of the bully was an overweight, overaggressive, not very intelligent boy who beat up on others to make himself feel better by proving his physical strength. There are still some of this type of bully out there, sure, but there's a much more dangerous bully type now.

Today's bullies are often popular, smart, charming to adults, and have many friends, even if their friendships are based on fear. They maintain their social status by making others objects of scorn and ridicule. To most people, they look like leaders. What bullies may not have is empathy, and that may be the most critical element differentiating them from kids with true leadership skills.

The thing that makes it so hard to deal with these types of bullies is that they're often hard to recognize, and hard for bystanders to stand up to. People like them. Teachers are amused by them. Coaches value them. Their social skills enable them to sweet-talk and appear innocent to adults, and their peers are terrified of standing up to them when they witness bullying behaviors because they could easily become the next targets. Whether they admit it or not, nearly all kids want to be popular. They want to have friends on the highest rung of the social ladder. They'll rarely contradict or confront a popular kid who's doing something wrong because that would make them "uncool" and likely to lose social status themselves.

Because of this, the popular bullies learn that they can get away with anything, and their empathy declines. They feel more and more powerful, and feel contempt for the less powerful kids. They're likely to repeat this pattern throughout life in their workplaces, towns, and families—teaching their kids how to climb the

BEHAVIORS AND TRAITS OF BULLIES

Bullies are more likely than other kids to do the following:

- Smoke
- Steal
- Lack empathy
- Be aggressive

- Vandalize property
- Use illegal drugs
- Cut classes
- Drop out of school

- Have aggressive friends
- Have high self-esteem[1]
- Be popular

 High self-esteem and popularity may be surprising qualities to see on a list of descriptions for bullies, but it's such an important piece of the equation. Some of the most manipulative bullies get away with it because of this; we don't pick them out as bullies because they don't fit our mind-set of what a bully looks like. If we're going to be successful in tackling this problem, we need to make this part of our mind-set. Some of the worst bullies have lots of friends and come across charming and attractive.

The negative behaviors become more problematic and rooted if bullying continues. And the more popular a bully becomes, the more he feels he can get away with, and the more he looks down on those he targets. We need to let popular bullies know that the ways they're getting power are unacceptable, and there are different ways to have positive power. Anything that increases a bully's social power is very bad news for those he targets.

social ladder so they can annihilate the "worthless" kids below them, too. That is part of the reason we have to deal with these issues early when they occur, because the longer kids get away with bullying, the less their empathy kicks in to stop these situations.

Why Are Kids Bullied?

Bullies will find any excuse to pick on a target. Too tall. Too short. Too fat. Too skinny. Too smart. Too stupid. Poor. An out-of-fashion haircut. Glasses. Braces. Different religion. Different race. Perceived homosexuality. Poor athletic ability. Flat-chested. Developing breasts early. A stutter. Teacher's pet. Shy. Disabled. Any type of perceived vulnerability will make a child a likelier target.

One factor remains pretty constant, though: The way a child responds to bullying events will determine whether those events repeat and escalate. The child who can laugh it off, walk away, and feel good about him- or herself anyway is not likely to become a long-term target. On the other hand, the likelihood of further attacks increases the more emotional the child becomes in reaction to the bullying. A child who gets very angry, cries, pouts, whines, or runs to a teacher is probably going to be harassed time and again.

That's the scary part of the bullying equation: In normal conflict, kids self-monitor. They can read each other's cues to know when they've crossed the line, and modify their behavior in response. That is, when two kids are pushing each other in the schoolyard and one kid starts to cry, the other will stop. The cue is received: "I've hurt someone," and acted upon with empathy: "I don't really want to hurt someone, so I'd better stop."

Take that same situation with a bullying dynamic, and the same cue is acted upon in an opposite manner. "I've hurt someone" is translated to: "Cool. I have more power. Let's see if I can really make this kid have a breakdown. This is fun!"

BEHAVIORS AND TRAITS OF TARGETS

Those who are targets of bullies are more likely than other kids to do the following:

- Develop social anxiety disorder as an adult[2]

- Have few friends

- Experience depression

- Dislike their peers

- Decline academically

- Have psychosomatic symptoms such as headaches, sleep difficulty, bed-wetting, and stomachaches[3]

- Think about or commit suicide, in extreme cases

 Some targets "act out" and get in trouble with authority figures because they have a hard time controlling their emotions, particularly if they're stressed out by being bullied. Bullies tend to be better at keeping their cool around authority figures, which often leads to the wrong person getting blamed (or both sharing the blame). Also, sometimes targets will drop out or purposely get themselves kicked out of an activity in the interest of self-preservation. Sadly, as many cases of school violence have proven, targets can also lose their empathy over time and become the bullies—retaliating with aggression.

What Bullies and Targets Have in Common

Both bullies and targets are more likely than other kids to witness violence between their parents at home.[4]

They're both more likely to have learning disabilities,[5] have trouble regulating their emotions, be maltreated by caregivers,[6] and abuse alcohol later in life.

Among boys, both bullies and targets are more likely to be obese than other kids.

Some people play both roles, too. A person who's been a target may turn and become a bully, trying to get back some social power. Targets may find someone lower on the social ladder (or younger—like a sibling) to pick on to relieve their own feelings of powerlessness.

Sibling Rivalry and Bullying

Kids test out their power and aggression with each other first, generally because there's a natural age imbalance, but how it develops and progresses is a function of parenting. If kids find out they can get away with it and aggression pays off, it will continue and turn into bullying.

Sibling rivalry is really just natural competition between siblings. Kids normally test out power issues with each other at home before they test them out with friends—it's more natural to do it at home, and easier to do with siblings than with parents (they don't bully their parents normally because there are clear consequences). It's not a problem unless sibling aggression crosses the line based on a parent's value system and parenting style.

Parents need to be really clear and up front about what is acceptable and what isn't. You can teach kids that conflict is acceptable, but that they need to use words that are not hurtful when they have an issue with their siblings, and that they may never harm someone physically. There must be consequences every time this is challenged.

Whenever you see kids getting too aggressive, you must step in and not let it escalate. Separate them, give them time to calm down,

BIRTH ORDER

There are no strong studies about how birth order affects bullying behavior. It can be argued that each role in the family dynamic could contribute to bully or target behavior, depending on how the family plays out those roles. An oldest child may bully a younger sibling out of jealousy—the oldest child once had the parents' exclusive attention, and wants to prove that he or she is still more powerful. A youngest child may learn to bully others because he or she had to "grow up fighting" for power. A middle child may feel lost in the family dynamic and bully others to draw attention—even if it's negative attention. And, conversely, any of them could fall into target roles just as easily.

and see if they can work out a way to share and be more positive with each other. Otherwise, sibling rivalry turns into bullying and kids take those bully and target roles into the classroom, sports, camp, and elsewhere.

Types of Bullying

There are three main types of bullying, with different probable effects.

Physical Bullying

This is the one that's easiest to identify. Punching, kicking, hair-pulling, bra-snapping, tripping, shoving someone into a locker—these can all be physical bullying episodes. Maybe surprisingly, this is usually the type of bullying with the fewest long-term scars for the target. Physical bullying has a beginning and an end. Once the incident is over, the bullying is over for a period of time. Depending on who wins the battle, the dynamic can shift immediately—the target can knock out the bully and suddenly gain power and brush off his target status. That's not exactly the ideal; most likely, the bully will just move on to someone else, and the target will either learn that fighting back is a way to gain power, or feel sick about the event. But it does sometimes stop the bullying.

Mark was a boy with a Catholic mother and a Jewish father, going to a Catholic prep school, when he found a Swastika taped to his locker. He'd been called "Jew boy" before and had been taunted about his religion, as well as his size (short and skinny). He usually just ignored the taunts, and today was no exception. He stuffed the Swastika picture into his coat pocket and forgot about it until his father found it later that night and demanded to know what happened.

The school took the bullying seriously—so seriously that the bully was suspended from school, even though it seemed that no one was happy about that idea. The boy was very popular, and once word got out that it was Mark's "fault" that the boy was kicked out, the bullying kicked into high gear.

He was in the locker room one day when a big athlete began chasing him around the room, threatening to kill him. Mark ran like his feet were on fire.

"Then I saw a half-open locker door in front of me," he says. "As I ran past it, I swung it hard behind me, and the kid fell to the ground. I just thought, 'Thank God,' because if not for that locker, that kid was going to kill me!"

And the bullying stopped.

But Mark reflects that he knew even then that this was a pretty screwy way to solve the problem. There's a danger in retaliation against a physical bully, of course. What if—and this is usually the case—the target can't beat the bully? If the target takes the bully up on his challenge, there's no guarantee whatsoever that the worst that's going to happen is a black eye or a few bruises.

We have to remember that a large number of schoolkids today may have greater access to and awareness of weapons, and may in fact be carrying them. And what looks like a one-on-one challenge can turn into a ten-on-one fight.

But in typical cases, physical wounds heal. It's when the physical bullying escalates or is combined with the other two forms of bullying that there's more risk of long-term damage.

Verbal Bullying

Taunting and name-calling fit into this category. Boys and girls are about equally likely to verbally bully and be bullied. Boys may bully boys or girls; girls typically bully only other girls.

What starts out as a taunt based on truth can easily morph into taunting based on whatever seems to get a rise from the target, regardless of whether or not there's any basis in reality. Maybe your child wears braces and kids call her "Metal Mouth." They see they get a reaction from her, so they see what else they can call her to drive her up a wall. Doesn't matter if she's pretty and they call her "Horse-Face," or if she's an A student and they call her stupid; they're not necessarily saying things they actually believe. They're just saying things that trigger strong emotional and behavioral responses. If they see that she gets really upset when they say she stuffs her bra, it makes no difference if they actually think so or not—they'll keep saying it because they see it upsets her.

They may find it even more fun to say ridiculous things they know aren't true, because it shows they can get a rise for no reason at all. No one actually believes the bully when he says, "I slept with your mom last night," or "You got those shoes out of the Dumpster," but his cronies will still crack up if it elicits a denial from the target.

And the target may tell the parent, "I just ignored him! I didn't do anything to provoke him and he still kept it up!" But what this usually means is, "I didn't say anything and I didn't cry." There are plenty of other ways the child may have reacted without even realizing it was a reaction—body language and facial expressions can be dead giveaways that a kid has been affected, and enough proof for the bully that the bullying was successful.

The target may have frowned or closed her eyes, folded her arms, bitten her lip, furrowed her eyebrows, run away, put her head down, looked away in an exaggerated manner, or any number of other cues that signify hurt or anger. Seeing the target really go berserk is the ultimate goal, but these little visual cues are enough to keep up the behavior to see if the target will eventually crack completely.

By now, most of us realize that the adage "Sticks and stones may break my bones, but words will never harm me" is a load of bull. The truth is that broken bones heal. Broken hearts are much harder to mend, and broken spirits can be lifetime handicaps.

And parents, no matter how many times you tell your kids, "You're smart and attractive," if all they hear from peers is "You're stupid and ugly," the latter is what they'll internalize. They don't believe you. You're biased—and besides, you're "old"! You're not going to negate the effects of verbal bullying just by assuring your child that the kids' words aren't true. Something has to change within the child to make the message sink in: Who cares what bullies think? I'm okay. I'm special. And who I am is perfectly likable.

Relational Bullying

Most popular among girls but also rampant among boys, the goal of this sort of bullying is social exclusion. It can take the form of gossip and exclusion from a lunch table, team, club, etc. If done on an ongoing basis, this form of bullying is likely the most hurtful and most damaging long-term. The targets don't just feel bullied by one person; they feel bullied by the whole peer group. It's a very sophisticated and manipulative form of bullying. It is also hitting a girl exactly where she's vulnerable—in her social likability.

Beyond about grade four, children's identity and self-esteem are dependent upon their peer groups far more than their families. When they feel shunned by and cut off from their peers, their self-esteem plummets and they feel like they have no "safe place." It's the exact opposite of what they want at that age, which is a feeling of belonging. Gossip, whether true or not, tends to be extremely hurtful and runs rampant in the young teen population.

Former friends may stop making eye contact and passing the target in hallways out of fear of being associated with this "social pariah." The target may hear giggling as she passes by, or watch people move away from her when she sits on a bench or on the school bus. Her trust in her peers is shattered, and she's likely to feel helpless and very alone.

It mimics the way a child feels when punished by being put in a "time out" corner. No words are necessary; the child is made to feel bad by being excluded from the family or group activities.

This is also what's at play when someone has a birthday party and invites everyone in the class . . . except one or two kids. That's just plain mean, and I encourage you as parents to make sure that your child doesn't contribute to making someone else feel excluded. The rule I find appropriate is: half or all, nothing in between. The child can invite everyone in the class, or half the people in the class (or less), but not a number in between those two.

As a parent, you may say this is ridiculous. "Why should I invite a kid who may be mean to my kid?" However, following along with the exclusion mind-set just teaches your child to do the same. They think, "Exclusion is acceptable if my parent allows it."

"I remember feeling like such a loser when everyone in my sixth grade class got invitations to a girl's party, except for me and one other girl," says a woman named Arisa. "I was a new girl in school, but it was a few months into the year, so she did know me. I spent the day looking around the room and thinking, "She thinks every person in this room is cooler than I am." Apparently, she kissed a boy for the first time there, so the party was a hot topic for months afterwards. I felt so isolated. And it was a self-fulfilling prophecy: the more insecure I felt about not being part of 'the group,' the less able I felt to make friends, which meant I just got more and more lonely and an easier target for teasing."

The Biggest Fear

In 2003, the National Girl Scouts Research Institute and Harris Interactive conducted a survey of 2,279 girls, ages eight to seventeen, to learn about their fears and concerns. What would you suppose the number 1 fear of preteen and teen girls would be? Terrorism? War? Disease? No . . .

Teasing.

Honestly, that's the top answer. "Being teased or made fun of" beat out every other fear, chosen by 41 percent of preteens and 22 percent of teens.[7]

RITA'S STORY

 I am very embarrassed to admit this, but I was a bully in primary school. I was particularly cruel to two fatter kids and got the majority of my class doing small jumps in time with each step the girls made.

I have agonized over this for a long time and have even tried to get in touch with them to apologize. I firmly believe that every action has a positive intent, so I spent a long time thinking about what I got out of this bullying. What was my positive intent? It's a strange question to ask yourself, but I think the answer is that these fatter kids were also the smarter ones. They were the ones who did well in math and spelling.

You see, because I'm dyslexic, my spelling is atrocious and I got the numbers in the wrong order as I copied them down from the board (I never got the right answer because I had the questions copied down wrong). Every single Thursday, I spent the first half of lunch rewriting all the spelling words

As girls get older, they have more physical fears (being attacked with a weapon, being forced to do something sexual), but teasing and gossip still weigh heavily on their minds.

Where the Power Lies

Statistics show that, on any given day in a classroom, bullies and targets usually constitute 15 percent of the population. That means that the other 85 percent of the children serve as observers in the bully dynamic. Interestingly enough, these observers may be the most powerful actors in the bully scenario, though all too frequently their power is passive, most often expressed as the absence of intervention or condemnation. Studies say that if bystanders do

I had wrong (the entire list), and every Friday, I spent almost the entire lunch rewriting, incorrectly more often than not, the entire dictation, while the "fat kids" got to play.

From an adult perspective, I believe the constant spelling punishments were, in a way, a form of bullying from the teachers. Perhaps I was evening the score by punishing the fat kids for not being good at sports. Perhaps my bullying was a way of making the world fair and just. Sports were the areas I excelled at; I won everything and was on the school team for every sports team we had. I was fit and I knew it. They were not being punished for not excelling at the area I excelled at, yet I was being punished for not being good at their areas of excellence. I wonder if my bullying was about fairness?

Once I got to high school, and the weekly spelling test ended, so did my bullying.

the "right" thing, they can reduce bullying incidents by at least 50 percent or more.

I have found that, more often than not, children want to do the right thing. My observations are echoed in a study of middle school students in Italy, where students watched videos enacting bullying scenarios: scenes where one person or a group bullied a target in school. After watching the video, the students filled out questionnaires about their opinions of the people in the video and who was to blame for the bullying. The researchers found that the children reported having positive feelings about the targets, and didn't generally blame the targets for what happened.[8]

However, even if they feel sympathy for the targets, when they don't act on it, they can become part of a group that permits or even encourages bullying behavior, and makes them enablers of the bullies and complicit in the victimization. Over time, even these kids who don't blame the targets begin to do so.

Learning Empathy

Rita, the former bully, is now a physical trainer who spends much of her professional life helping overweight people get in shape. She was sort of a mix between the "old-school" bully and the newer, popular bully type. She had plenty of self-esteem in certain areas (she knew she was a good athlete and pretty and powerful), but she had no "classroom self-esteem," as she calls it. So much of her life was wrapped up in those spelling and math tests, and she didn't feel good about herself in an academic sense, so she bullied kids to feel better about herself.

"I didn't realize the pain I was causing the two girls; I just knew that being cruel to them somehow made me feel good," she says. "Someone should have taken me aside and explained how my actions made the girls feel, asked how I would have liked to feel like that, and then when I agreed I would not have liked it, they could have asked me not to do it."

Part of the problem for Rita is that no one seemed to offer her any empathy for her own problem. Her mother was a journalist who had no idea why her daughter couldn't just sound out the words, and tried bribing her to get better test grades. Rita became exasperated because it wasn't for lack of trying that she was failing. She felt she was being punished for something beyond her control, like punishing a blind person for not being able to see. So she grew increasingly bitter and aggressive.

"If the focus was taken off this one thing I could not do, this thing that was dominating my life, then I would not have felt the need to punish those who were both good at what I could not do, and bad at what I was good at," she says.

Social Dominance Theory

According to Social Dominance Theory, there is a hierarchy in all group situations. Someone's always going to be at the top of the ladder and someone's always going to be on the bottom.

Now, of course, no one wants to be the one on the bottom—therefore, they want someone *else* to be on the bottom. This is part of what explains the "do-nothing" bystanders and even those who participate in bullying despite their consciences. As long as people continue to shun someone else, they're safe from being the biggest loser in school—a title no one wants to claim.

A man named Daniel says that his son, a second grader at the time, had become a target of the class bully, a boy who'd been left back about three times and was a lot bigger than his classmates. Daniel told his son to ignore the kid. "It didn't work for him, but a week or so later, while sitting at the dinner table, my son proudly announced that he'd been able to figure out how to handle Henry: 'I told Henry that if he would stop beating on me, I would help him beat up the other kids!'

"Needless to say, we quickly informed him this wasn't an option."

Daniel's son was able to talk his way out of it and even reason with the bully that he should probably quit it now before he got to high school and wasn't the biggest kid in school anymore and lines of people were waiting to pound on him. But you can see the logic in his initial thought—out of self-preservation, he was willing to help the bully terrorize someone else to get himself out of trouble!

Standing up for someone who's on the bottom carries a big risk. It means that you could take that person's place. You could look like a fool, could be laughed at and picked on and isolated. It takes a person with fairly high social standing to intervene and stop bullying alone. But if a group of kids take a stand, the bully is less likely to continue. It's much less appealing to pick on a target who has a buffer of friends or allies.

Friendship Groups

The treatment and the cure for most bullying is friendship. When children feel so marginalized that they withdraw from social contact, you've hit a really dangerous point. Some children, because of special needs or poor social skills, have extreme trouble making friends. Others just lack the confidence that anyone might like them, possibly because they've already been bullied and no one has stood up for them (therefore making the children believe that everyone hates them).

When a child develops the social skills to become "friend-eligible," that child has picked up an important bully shield. Even if the child's friends also get teased, they can still have a sense of belonging and can still serve as modulators for the effects of the bullying.

There's often a spillover effect once kids figure out that they're friend-eligible. A child who had no friends at school may find friends at summer camp or in a club. At that point, the child realizes that he or she is worthy of friendship and has the ability to make friends: "Hey, I'm not a loser after all!" So the following year, it's more likely that he will also find friends at school or not take on the belief that he is a loser in every situation.

Long-Term Consequences of Bullying

Even when the bullying doesn't end in broken bones or death, it can have long-standing consequences for all involved—the target, the bully, those who assist the bully or the target, and the observers.

WHAT HAPPENS IN HIGH SCHOOL?

Julie Rusby and colleagues from the Oregon Research Institute followed 223 middle school students through their high school years to find out what effect peer harassment had on their development. In 2005, the researchers published their results. They found that those who experienced frequent harassment were prone to become antisocial and aggressive, and that verbal harassment during the middle school years increased the likelihood of a teenager's alcohol use during high school almost threefold.[9]

You may have seen talk shows where formerly bullied kids come to say "look at me now" to their old tormentors. There's something so sad about the fact that the bullies are still on these adults' minds, still influencing them. Most can recall every humiliation, every taunt, and even twenty or thirty years later, they're still trying to measure up and gain the bullies' approval. Often, these are women who've had plastic surgery to "correct" a flaw the bullies picked on, or men who've become bodybuilders in response to jabs from bullies who saw them as weak or nerdy.

"Childhood is what you spend the rest of your life trying to overcome," says Sandra Bullock in the movie *Hope Floats*. For many bullied kids, that's about right. A three-year study by the UK charity Kidscape revealed that adults who were bullied in school are up to seven times more likely to attempt suicide than those who weren't bullied.[10] They're also more likely to continue playing the victim role throughout their adult lives, getting bullied in the workplace, in romantic relationships, in their families, and in their neighborhoods.

Or they may "snap" and become the aggressors, now that they've learned that violence gives people power. The U.S. Secret Service surveyed the attackers in 37 recent school shootings, and discovered that more than two-thirds of them believed they had been bullied.[11] The desire for revenge doesn't end when school lets out, though: In Japan in 2003, a thirty-four-year-old man learned how to make a bomb on the Internet, and planted it at the home of his former high school bully. He was badly burned when the bomb exploded early, and was later sentenced to twelve years in prison.[12] That kind of anger was stewing inside this man for nearly *twenty years* after he was bullied.

As for the bullies, a study from the University of British Columbia found that 60 percent of children identified as bullies in grades six to nine wind up with a criminal record by the time they are twenty-four.[13]

Then there are those who sided with the bullies even against their true feelings. Those people get to live with that guilt as long as they live.

"My older brother, Charlie, was retarded and always subject to bullying," says Jim Fox. "About fifteen years ago, while calling on a business issue, a customer recognized my name. He asked if I'm the Jim Fox that went to Downey High School in Modesto. I am. He asked about Charlie, and I explained he'd passed away some years ago. The man began to weep, and apologized for the treatment he'd subjected my brother to so many years earlier.

"He explained his own son suffered from Down syndrome, and every school day was torment for him. He apologized again, and said he had always felt sorry for my brother but had gone along with the taunting so that he could fit in. After the man hung up, I realized the power of bullying and the incredible peer group pressure it exerts. This man himself has gone through life with a birth defect—a missing right hand—yet he bullied my brother 'to fit in.'"

It's never too late to reach out and try to make amends and apologize for prior wrongdoings. Although it was too late for this man to apologize directly to Charlie, it was still something his brother appreciated hearing. In many cases, it can help a target to heal, even many years later.

The Good News

The good news is that bullying doesn't have to have a traumatic end. Clay Aiken, a multi-platinum-selling singer from *American Idol*, says that bullies verbally harassed him throughout his middle school years because of his clothes, hair, and glasses. Sometimes the bullying was physical, too, with his tormentors delighting in giving him "wedgies" and thrashing him with dodgeballs.

Fortunately for Clay, his experience didn't manifest into bitterness. It manifested into empathy. He learned to develop self-esteem based on his talents and the love from his friends and family. Before his rise to fame, he was a special education teacher who tried to instill that same self-esteem in the kids he worked with. Now his charity foundation helps the families of children with developmental disabilities, particularly autism. Clay never became the bodybuilder—in fact, he retained just about all the traits the bullies picked on—but his "geek chic" style didn't bother the millions of fans who now support his career.

Kate Winslet says she was bullied so badly for being overweight that she went through a period where she became dangerously anorexic, but she's now a role model for "normal" women who are thrilled to see a curvaceous woman making it big in Hollywood. Sandra Bullock had such physical and verbal bullying troubles that a guidance counselor visited her mom at home because she just didn't know what to do to help anymore. Singer and actress Brandy says she tried to "buy" friendships with her lunch money after girls pulled her hair and teased her for being too skinny and not pretty enough. Obviously these women have moved past the bullying in their lives—but none of them have forgotten it.

Bullied kids tend to be sensitive, caring individuals who are often creative and original. If bullied kids get the help they need to overcome their troubles, they can actually become more empathetic to the plights of others, more self-confident, and more likely to teach tolerance to their own kids one day. In fact, the very kids who tend to get bullied often have the potential to become excellent leaders and highly successful individuals.

But to get there, they first need to move beyond the crisis and develop true self-love and self-confidence.

It's Not a Tragedy:
It's an Opportunity

One key point I'd like to impress upon parents is that—strange as it may sound now—there can be something really positive about bullying.

Think about the times when you've felt really good about yourself. Go ahead: Think of a few examples of times when you felt proud of yourself.

Got it?

Most of the experiences that really build our confidence and self-worth aren't just about winning. They're about being on the bottom and finding our way up. Does that fit your examples? Maybe you were proud of a time you overcame an addiction, or passed a difficult test, or stood up for yourself to a boss who terrified you, or survived a life-threatening situation.

That's the whole secret to developing real self-esteem. It's not about heaping praise on someone; it's about those times when they were really down and figured out how to pull themselves out of it.

When they faced tremendous challenges and learned they were strong enough, smart enough, brave enough, good enough to overcome the odds.

So the first attitude adjustment I'd like you as a parent or caretaker to make is that finding out your child is being bullied or is a bully isn't a reason to get hysterical. That's the tendency—no parents want to see their children suffer, of course, and they can get pretty fired up when they find out their children are being targeted. I've talked to hundreds of parents whose first reaction is to cry, scream, yank the kid out of school, threaten to sue the school . . .

The truth is that your child is going to take cues from you. If you're all worked up, the child will get all worked up (and that's the last thing you want because it'll just fuel the bully). If you rush in to shield the child and save the day, the child learns to be helpless. No lesson learned. No opportunity for growth.

Except in really extreme cases, the goal should always be for the child to have control of the solution. Of course parents and other adults can and should help, but not take over and leave the child out of the plan. It's important for the child to feel that he or she did something positive to get out of the situation.

That's the only reason I can continue doing the work I do. If all I saw was misery and victimization, I could never be a bully coach and still be a functioning and happy person. But instead, what I see is opportunity. I know that if I can help children learn the skills they need to stop being bullied, they're going to gain self-confidence that will be with them for the rest of their lives. They're going to feel like they've gone from being losers to being winners, and that feeling is the real power that can propel them to great heights.

Yes, bullying is something to take seriously, and no, I don't expect you to shout "Hooray!" when you find out your child is being victimized. But I ask you to look at it as a challenge with great potential rewards. Teaching a child resilience is like giving that child keys to a magic kingdom. The world becomes brighter, the impossible feels possible, and future challenges don't feel so hopeless.

So let's examine this opportunity and use it for all it's worth. Know that even if the situation looks grim right now, there's a real possibility that your child will grow from this and become stronger and happier than ever before. The greatest victories are the ones we struggle to achieve.

TWO

The **Bullyproofing** Prescription

Bullying is meant to humiliate, and it does its job quite well. Often, bullied kids are so embarrassed that they don't even want to tell their parents. They may be afraid that the parent will tell them never to speak to a bullying kid again, think less of them, that the parent will side with the bullies, make light of the problem, take action that will humiliate them further, or worse: not believe them. So how can you find out what's going on?

Three steps make up the bullyproofing prescription: Recognize, Act, and Preserve (RAP).

Phase One: Recognize

Before we can tackle the bullying problem, you'll need to recognize the problem and find out exactly what's happening. The real challenge parents face in the crisis phase—and unfortunately, events are likely to unfold in this manner—comes when your child, out of shame, guilt, fear, or some combination of all three, doesn't share with you what's been going on until the crisis is so acute she feels completely overwhelmed. At this point, the way you react can have a big impact.

Recognizing the problem entails detailed discussions with the child and appropriate reactions so the child will trust that you're on his team and able to help. Use the following steps:

1. Read cues to initiate a talk.

Choosing the right time for heart-to-heart conversations is crucial. The time to talk to your child about bullying behaviors is not when he's watching his favorite television show, playing a video game, or trying to go to sleep. Ideally, you'll know it's the right time to talk because the child comes to *you* and tells you about the problem. This is more common with younger kids, but even then, it doesn't always happen.

Don't jump to take it personally if a child doesn't talk to you about these kinds of problems. It may have something to do with how you've reacted to other problems in the past, or it may have nothing to do with you—it could just be that the child is embarrassed, wants to pretend it never happened, wants to figure out how to deal with it on his own, is too upset to talk about it right now, or any number of other reasons.

If the child is just sitting around looking glum, that's a time to approach. If confidentiality isn't an issue (no other siblings at the table), during dinner might be an okay time. In the car while driving home from school or an activity is an ideal time. If you don't seem to have a perfect time built in, make one. Ask the child to help you with dinner preparation, or setting the table. Ask the child to come with you to pick up dessert.

2. Help the child open up.

Always start the conversation on a positive or neutral note that doesn't have to do with bullying. The key point here is for you to be relaxed. If you're uptight, whatever conversation you begin will be seen as covering up some other agenda you have. Some good conversation-starters include:

Did you learn anything interesting today?

What did you do in recess today?

Did you hear about . . . that I heard on the radio or saw on TV today?

Did you do anything fun with your friends today?

What was your favorite thing that you did today?

You can ease your way into the tougher questions, but begin by letting the child see that you are engaged, interested, and ready to listen before jumping into "risky" territory. Then you can ask about bullying experiences.

If the child says, "I don't want to talk about it," respect that and ask the child to come back to you when he *is* ready. If he doesn't come back to talk about it, try again after a meal, or the following day. Don't get threatening or angry about the reluctance to talk. Forcing a child to talk is going to backfire, simple as that.

3. React calmly.

This is one of the most important parts of the whole equation: You need to stay cool, no matter what comes out of your child's mouth. From the moment that child begins opening up, you're being tested. You have to pass the test, or there may not be a next time. One of the main points is that your child wants to see that you won't "freak out." (Parents are known for shutting down the conversation when they "freak out.")

Don't react with alarm, anger, or overt anxiety. *Don't* appear upset or fearful. This will push your child's sense of crisis into overdrive.

You are a very tall person with a lot of power in that child's mind. Your main job right now is to look sympathetic and listen. Keep your intense emotions to yourself or wait until you calm down. Take a couple of deep breaths until you feel at ease. If you open up conversation with lots of intensity, you can expect to get back lots of intensity. It's tough enough for your child to open up without having to worry about your reaction.

Most parents think they'll react calmly . . . until the situation actually arises. Then it *actually* goes more like this:

PARENT: So, what happened?

CHILD: This kid named Bobby kicked me on the bus today, and I fell down and dropped my notebook, so his friend picked it up and ripped up the pages and threw them out the window. Then Bobby told me if I said anything, he would beat me up after school.

PARENT: They did *what*? He *kicked you*?! Didn't the bus driver say anything? Who are these kids? I want their parents' phone numbers. How dare they! Is this the same kid who ripped your backpack last month? I'm going to straighten him out! HE SHOULDN'T EVEN BE ALLOWED IN SCHOOL! THAT JERK IS GONNA PAY FOR THIS!

This is the point when your kid decides it was a big mistake to say anything and vows never to open his mouth again. Instead, you could just say, "Were you hurt? Are you okay?" You can scream in the car, alone, later.

4. Use active listening techniques.

One of the best ways to show a child you're listening and understanding is to mirror back her feelings. Resist all urges to interrupt with pointed questions, advice, or blame. Instead, just sit there and listen and occasionally nod and interpret what feelings you think she's expressing.

For example, if she says, "No one let me play with them at recess today," you could say, "Boy, you must have felt lonely." If she says someone tripped her in the hall, you could say, "That must have been so embarrassing to you." Then she can agree and let you know you're on the right track—or disagree and correct you about how she really felt. ("I didn't feel lonely. I felt mad!") Remember, if you make a comment about her feelings or what you think she's feeling, you're on the right track!

5. Take breaks.

You don't have to solve everything right now. Again, watch for cues. If your child is shutting down, repeating himself, getting overemotional, losing focus, showing frustration, or not listening well, take a break. This is a weighty issue for your child, and he may be able to handle only a little bit at a time. Say something like, "Why don't we take a break and talk some more later? We'll come up with a plan and somehow we'll find a way to help." Always end on a hopeful note.

GENDER DIFFERENCES
WHEN SPEAKING TO YOUR CHILDREN

Boys are generally more sensitive than girls about exposing weaknesses in themselves and may be reluctant to do it, so before having one-to-one conversations with them, make sure you let them know that it's okay to talk without fear of being in trouble. If you approach your son with any hint of a negative tone, he'll likely shut down. Even if he was victimized, he may feel guilty about not being able to handle it himself, or he may worry that you'll yell at him for any actions he has taken so far (like striking back or calling the bully names). He may feel inadequate and worry that you'll ridicule him for failing to solve the problem. He may not want to tell you that the teacher yelled at both of them for fighting—even if your son was innocent. Let boys know that even if you suspect they may be having problems, or getting into trouble, you trust them, and that even if they messed up, it will be okay. Boys don't want to show vulnerability, so they may use anger or bad behavior to cover up feelings of frustration or vulnerability.

6. Praise.

Similarly, you'll want to end each conversation with positive reinforcement for the child:

I'm really proud of you for talking about this.

I'm really proud of you for being so brave.

I'm really proud of you for the way you handled yourself.

I'm really proud of you for being mature.

I'm really proud of you for trying out something new.

I'm really glad you told me, even though it's not easy to talk about.

Girls need to feel valued before they will open up, and the best way to demonstrate that is by telling them something that you admire about them: You really like the way she can be a friend, or kind to her sister or brother. Let her know that you value her and that you know she is a good person. When bullying is verbal or relational, girls don't always call it "bullying" and may not expect you to take it seriously, even if it's consuming her thoughts. Exclusion and meanness may be part of what she thinks is normal. This is why it's important to tell her that you do want to hear her experiences and will believe her and take them seriously. When you ask a girl questions, she may avoid answering by taking the "avoidance" way out, saying, "I don't know." This is really an excuse to get out of a conversation, so tell her, "I know if you take some time and think about it, you can come up with something." This doesn't allow her to get off the hook so easily and shows her that you care about these issues and won't avoid them yourself.

How to Talk to Your Child about Bullying

The way you approach the subject will differ depending on whether you're talking to a boy or girl, and what age your child is. In the following sections, you will find your child's gender and age, and the particular approach that will be most effective.

Up to Second Grade

With younger children, you need to take the lead in terms of managing the situation. It'll be up to you to give your child the language: the right things to say to the bully, or the right behaviors to use. It'll also be up to you to speak with teachers or the principal if the bullying continues. Don't expect your child to formulate a plan at this point, or to have many worthwhile suggestions about what to do about the problem.

They're looking for your reassurance that everything is going to be okay, and they get scared if you overreact. Think about the toddler who falls down, but looks to the parent before reacting. The child falls, then checks to see what the parent does—if the parent looks horrified and yells or rushes over to sweep the child up, the child cries. If the parent smiles and says, "Oops!" or something similar, the child is less likely to cry and more likely to pick himself up and keep going. In both cases, the child isn't actually hurt, but maybe just a bit shaken, and he doesn't know how to feel, so he tries to figure it out based on how *you* feel. If you're freaked out, then he knows to be upset!

Third Through Sixth Grade

This is when concrete thinking and cognitive development improve, and kids are more able to begin making sense of their own power in relation to others. Therefore, this is the time to include them on brainstorming sessions to come up with a plan to address the problem. It's good to ask, "What do you think about this?" or "How about if we try that?" or "Do you have any ideas for what you could say if he picks on you again?"

Confidentiality is more important at this stage, so if you talk to school, camp, or sports officials, make sure they know that they are not to inform the bully or anyone else that you or your child "tattled." "Reporting" problems is a much more useful word here, and that has to do with getting kids into a situation that helps them feel emotionally and/or physically safe and out of danger.

This is the age where school avoidance becomes more common, so you need to make sure you're working on teaching your child skills to be resilient against school bullies before the problem gets severe. If you simply rush to the school to get the bully punished, your child hasn't learned how to deal with the problem in the future. Use lots of role-playing and examples to talk through the types of incidents your child may face and how to react.

Seventh Grade and Beyond

Kids at this age are watching your reactions very carefully— they're noticing your body language, your tone, your words, and whether or not they match each other. If they feel like you're judging them at all, or that you don't "get it," or that you're overreacting, it's over. So one good tactic to use early on is to relate your own experiences with bullying to let your child understand that you've been there and done that.

You don't need to go on at great length, but try to come up with a similar situation you remember from your own youth when you or someone you cared about was targeted by bullies, and validate your child's feelings by talking about how it made you feel at the time—humiliated, scared, lonely, stupid, whatever. Help your child normalize the experience. Many teens and preteens already feel like outcasts; being the targets of bullies just makes that worse. If you can make it safe to relate to you and let them feel like they're not alone in their experiences and feelings, it'll be much more likely that they'll realize you're someone they can come to when they need to talk.

Keep in mind that they care more about what their peers think at this point than what you think, and that's developmentally normal. Even so, however, they still want your support. You have to take a backseat unless the situation has escalated to a major safety concern, but be there to talk and to help the child figure out what to do.

The last thing your child wants at this point is for you to make her feel like a totally powerless loser, which is just what you'll do if you rush in to save the day against her wishes. It'll make her think that even you think she's weak and helpless. If she already feels like her peers don't respect her, it could be really depressing for her to believe that her parents don't, either. So even if she doesn't succeed at figuring out what works right away, it's a better strategy to just keep listening and offering suggestions rather than trying to handle the situation for her. And if nothing you say helps, just say, "We'll keep working on this until you come up with a way that helps."

Questions to Ask

I have developed a set of questions to help you create a productive conversation with your child. Instead of trying to pull teeth out to get your child to respond, ask questions that lead to deeper responses. You can modify these questions based on the information you want to obtain from your child.

WHAT NOT TO ASK

How was your day at school today?

What did you do today?

Was everything okay?

Although this is usually a parent's first instinct, these questions will get you nowhere. How did you answer when your parents asked you these questions?

"Fine." "Nothing." "Yeah."

Better Questions

The following questions are designed to help parents uncover specific bullying-related behavior that their children may be involved in or observe in others. By asking behavior-specific questions designed around the places where your child may be bullied, you can find out the information you need to effectively counter that bullying.

You can tailor these questions to your specific situation. Good questions address specific behavior and are not open-ended. Try to think about the information you want to obtain. Maybe it is a general set of questions about how each part of your child's social life is going.

Let's take a school example. Begin addressing the first part of the day when children go to school. If your child goes to school on a bus, you would begin by addressing the specifics on the school bus. If there is a bus ride, it's essential to ask about it because bullying happens when supervision is lean and supervision may be absent on the bus. If the child walks to school, you'll want to find out if anyone greets her or if she ever takes a different path to avoid anyone.

Think about those places where your child may be with less supervision and ask questions about those areas: recess (playing a game or sports), lunch, bus, hallway, locker room, bathroom, in line, walking to and from school, or waiting for pickup.

By thinking about those places where your child may be away from supervision, you can begin to think how to specifically address those areas. These may be better questions to ask your child to get specific answers and information that may alert you to a problem:

- Who do you talk to on the bus?

- Do you sit with the same children every day?

- Has this child ever sat with someone else?

- Who did you sit with that day?

- Have you ever sat alone?

- What would you do if that child were out sick, or who would you sit with if you had to find another child?

- Does anyone ever get picked on, called names, or teased during the bus ride?

- Does this ever happen to you?

- Do you ever do this to someone else?

- Does anyone ever get knocked out of his seat on the bus?

- Has this ever happened to you?

- Do kids act like there are assigned seats and has anyone ever challenged that?

- Has anyone ever been mad at you for sitting in his or her seat? What did that person do to you?

- Who do you eat lunch with every day?

- Does it ever happen that your group isn't there, and if so, who would you join for lunch?

- Do you have someone to play with during recess?

- Who did you play with at recess today?

- Do you notice if anyone is being teased, picked on, or left out at lunch or recess?

- Does anyone ever get left out of a game at recess? Or not have the ball passed to him on purpose?

- Does this ever happen to you?

- Who would you tell if it did happen to you?

If the child reveals that incidents like this do happen to him . . .

- Do your friends know?

- Have you ever asked them to help you?

- Have you spoken to anyone in school about this?

- What adults do you feel safe with in school?

- What kids do you feel safe with in school?

- Has anyone who has seen this reported it to an adult?

- Does your school have any way that you can report this without feeling like it will make things worse?

The early questions about who he sits with on the bus, who he plays with at recess, etc., are meant to check whether your child has friends around in the places where bullying thrives. A child who has friends has a buffer. If the child is being bullied despite having friends around, these friends may need help understanding how to help.

Asking whether your child has ever witnessed bullying may be easier for your child to answer than if you begin by asking if she's ever been a target. Once she's talking about the subject and has seen that your reaction is compassionate rather than judgmental, she may feel less embarrassed to tell you about her own experiences.

The third set of questions establishes how comfortable your child and her peers feel about seeking help from others. You may discover that she's already told a teacher, or that she didn't know she should.

You may discover that she would rather eat mud than "tattle." Your objective during this stage is not to lecture your child or convince her of what she should do, but merely to gather information.

Your child may talk freely about some questions and not others. Be sure to watch your child's facial expressions, tone, and change of emotion when you ask specific questions. Avoidance of some questions or hesitation when answering can alert you to a possible problem. You don't want to bully your child to answer what she doesn't feel comfortable answering, but please take note, and refer back to any question or response that seemed to make your child uncomfortable. It is only your persistence and determination, caring, and follow-through that may get the information you seek. It may not come the first time around.

Asking these questions on an ongoing basis also allows you to check for the reliability of your children's answers. Responses that are vague or are different from before can alert you to a potential issue that may be uncomfortable for them. If you suspect something may not be right, reassure your kids that you are there for them, and open to talk when they are ready. This allows them to trust their gut and you, so when the time is right, you may hear what you need to fit the puzzle pieces together.

When You Can't Wait

Sometimes you can't wait for the child to come around. If you already have evidence that something's seriously wrong (the child is coming home with torn clothes, or continually fakes illnesses, or you've seen threatening e-mails, for example), you'll have to take a more forward approach.

"I see a problem here and I can't let this continue," you might say. Talk about the evidence you've seen and ask for details in a nonthreatening way.

If I allow my child to keep coming home with bruises or missing lunch money without talking to me about it, the message I'm giving is that I'm unwilling to stick with him and get the problem solved. Even if the child doesn't want to open up, I have to role-model the appropriate behavior—I have to show that what's happening is *not* acceptable and that I care enough to intervene. If the child is at least ten years old, I have to become a polite pest until I get the story.

"Because I care, I'm not backing down from this," you could say. "I will not act on anything you tell me until we come up with a plan together, but I know there's an issue and I love you too much to ignore it."

If the child won't open up, take a ten-minute break. Tell him he can go think about it and you'll come back to talk. If he's not ready to deal with it then, give him thirty minutes and try again. Let him know you're not going away.

For children under ten years old, you may have to get the information elsewhere—possibly from the school, others who may have observed the behavior, or friends' parents.

For older children who remain reluctant to talk, suggest that the child write you a note if that's easier. Promise to keep the note confidential and even to destroy it after you've read it if that's what the child wants.

If Your Child Is a Target

If you learn that your child is a target, you must create an environment that is nonthreatening and safe for him or her. Accomplish this by remembering these steps:

- **Listen to his feelings** in a nonjudgmental manner. If you react with a strong emotional outburst, you may shut your child down because he will fear you, like he fears the bully. Make sure that you are in a calm place when you make time to listen, or he may observe that your feelings are overly intense, and shut down.

- **Try to gather information** about the specifics of the incident(s). Documentation becomes a powerful tool when you have to deal with the school or another parent. Try to note the specific times that incidents occurred, and who was present when the incident happened (adults and children).

- **Never blame your child** for being bullied. Bullying is a behavior that no one deserves, and if you blame your child, she will feel diminished as a person, similar to how the bully made her feel. Even if you believe your child was provoking this behavior, do not blame her. Do not suggest that she's "too sensitive" or "too emotional," or anything else that implies that you think she's weak. In time, you'll need to help your child manage her own behavior. The way you do this is to problem-solve with her, even if she cannot come up with answers. The critical variable is that if children have exhausted their own resources, they may have to see that involving an adult with more power is the next solution until they can find a way on their own to manage these issues.

- **Empower your children** by helping them come up with a plan. Ask your children (grades two and beyond, generally) what help you can give them. You can role-play how to stand up to a bully if they feel safe, become a good reporter to a teacher or aide, enlist a friend, or avoid the bully situation. For children who are younger, you may need to call the school and speak with the teacher, so someone in power can look out for your child.

- **Don't bully your child** into making a choice he's not ready to make. For example, if you tell your child to stand up straight, look a bully in the eye, and say, "Stop it, this is bullying" before he's ready, you can make him feel *less* powerful. Your child may feel like you're bullying him. Try to encourage your children, but at a pace that works for them. Remember that not all children can ever make this choice based on their comfort level and temperament. Some children need other peers or adults to help and cannot be direct with a peer they're afraid of.

- **Reward your child** for speaking with you by praising her. Specific praise like "I'm so proud of you for telling me about this bullying situation, and now you've developed a plan of action" works best because she knows specifically what she did that empowered her, and allows her to be proud of her behavior. Nonspecific praise, such as "Good work," doesn't provide enough clarity for children to understand that certain behavior leads to praise and positive power for them.

If Your Child Is a Bully

It can be very difficult to hear that your child is a bully, and most parents' natural instinct is to deny it. ("My child would never do that.") Try to be aware of your own emotions, and to resist the urge to find someone else to blame or a way to excuse the behavior.

- **Denial won't help.** If you deny that your child has responsibility for bullying, your ability to change the situation is gone. Accept that the possibility exists that your child has done something to hurt someone else, and address it as thoroughly as possible.

- **Take it seriously.** Even if they accept that something undesirable may have occurred, many parents try to minimize the issue. Making it seem like no big deal, or that other people are overreacting or being too sensitive, will teach your child that hurting others is not a big deal to you. It can also add to her scorn, because now she can add "oversensitive" to the list of reasons to bully people.

- **Squelch your anger.** If you're angry, your child will shut down. Talk to your child in a calm way, at a time when your emotions have settled. Try to understand the specifics of an incident from your child's perspective without raising your voice.

- **Keep your child focused on accountability.** "I don't want to hear about what the other kid did right now," you might say. "I want to hear about what you did. No matter what you think happened, how did you handle it? Help me understand what you did that caused this kid to feel bad."

- **Encourage empathy.** Once you've collected information about the incident, it's time to ask your child to turn it around and put herself in the other child's shoes. "When you did that, how did that child feel? How would you feel if someone did that to you?" Ask her to take the position of the other child.

- **Brainstorm restitutions.** "When you've done something to hurt someone else, you have to show that you're sorry. What can you do to make this child feel like you're sorry, and that you know what you did was wrong? How can you make her feel better?" It's not enough just to talk about it; your child needs to do something positive. This might be writing a letter to the target, calling her, having a meeting in person, and/or standing up for her with others who are picking on her.

- **Decrease the amount of aggression in your child's life.** If your child is prone to bullying behavior, do what you can to get rid of bad examples. Limit violent television and video games, make sure that you argue with your significant other in private if you need to argue, pay attention to the lyrics of the music he listens to.

- **Ask for a peer mentor.** Sometimes, bullies are not savvy about how to make friends without using bullying. If you think it would be helpful, ask an authority figure if he can assign a peer mentor or a "big brother/big sister" type of student to help your child figure out better ways to socialize.

Be Fully Present

One of the surest ways to know that your child will tell you when something is really wrong is to be there for the silly problems.

As adults, we know that most of the "problems" kids go on and on about are . . . well, really trivial. And some kids are phenomenally long-winded miniature drama queens and kings. They want to share every little detail of every silly thing someone said or did. What they really want, though, is your attention (or someone's).

But it doesn't feel trivial for your child at that moment. Your child probably doesn't yet know what "big" problems feel like, so the little ones feel really important. If you let on that you think your child's problems are stupid, or don't matter, you're sending the message that you don't care about your child's feelings . . . and that can come back to haunt you when there *is* a real problem, like bullying.

So vow to yourself that when your child comes to you with a problem—no matter how silly you think it is—you'll drop everything and be fully present. You'll listen, and sympathize, and offer suggestions if needed, and try your best not to make judgmental statements that minimize or trivialize your child's feelings. You can try to help your child put something in perspective, but do so

without smirks, eye rolls, throwing your arms in the air, interrupt-
ing, and so on.

A fourth-grade girl had a friend in the neighborhood who
argued over everything. These two girls were actually friends—but
they were constantly fighting over nothing in particular, and her
mother had to hear about it every day. "She said this" and "she
said that" and "she called me this" could take up twenty minutes a
day, and none of it mattered for more than a day, because by the
next day, they were fighting over a whole new set of nonsense.

The mother came up with a "rule" for the girls to enact: They
were allowed to fight only on Wednesdays.

The crazy thing is that it actually worked for them. The two
girls agreed to save up their arguments and really have it out every
Wednesday. A couple of times in the beginning, the mother would
hear them arguing outside, and she'd call out, "Girls . . . it's not
Wednesday yet," and that would actually stop the fighting in its
tracks. Soon thereafter, the girls began saying it to each other, and
eventually it became an inside joke. By Wednesday, neither girl
could ever remember the things they wanted to argue about the
rest of the week. What the girls developed were some boundaries
together.

By putting in the "sweat equity" of listening to all that silliness
and helping her child solve a smaller problem, this mother gained
her child's trust and was much more likely to be called upon if the
child had a more serious problem later—whether with bullies, or
any number of other issues.

If You Already Blew It

If your child used to talk to you, but now shuts down when
talking about emotional things, it could very well just be a product
of "growing pains" (young children talk openly to their parents

much more than preadolescents and adolescents do), or the child may be humiliated about something, or it may be that you've reacted badly in the past or given off the wrong signals without meaning to.

Try to remember how you've handled these problems before. Now try to see your reactions from a child's point of view:

- **Anger.** In all likelihood, you're angry with the bully, the school, the camp, the bus driver, the kids who said nothing . . . you're probably angry with everyone *but* your kid. The problem is that young kids don't differentiate well. They see anger and they think, "I made her angry." They don't want you to be angry.

- **Blame.** The moment you start asking things like, "What did you do to provoke it?" or "Did you do something to make him mad?" you've already "sided" with the bully, in your child's mind. You've raised doubts about your trust in your child and put him on the defensive. There are ways to ask about the child's behavior without bringing up any sort of blame assignment.

- **Broken confidentiality.** It's hard to recover from this if you've ignored your child's wishes before and gone to a teacher, principal, bully's parents, etc., with the child's private concerns. The child is unlikely to share private information with you again, knowing that you could make the situation worse.

- **Too much concern.** Some parents can be so worried about a bullying situation that they make a child feel even worse about it. Even after the crisis has passed, a parent can keep harping on it, and making the child feel like there's something to continue worrying about. Too much babying can make the child feel even more powerless than she already felt.

If you now realize that you've reacted like this in the past, it's time to make amends. Children appreciate it when parents admit they've been wrong. It's a good idea to go to your child and say, "You know, I let my emotions get the best of me. I was so upset because I don't ever want you to be hurt, and I think I overreacted. I didn't mean to sound so angry. I'll do a better job next time you want to talk to me."

Be aware not only of your words, but also your tone and your body language. Here are the cues to watch out for in yourself:

Positive	Negative
▪ Arms and legs uncrossed	▪ Arms crossed
▪ Sitting or lying down at the child's level	▪ Standing over child
	▪ Looking away frequently
▪ Making eye contact	▪ Shaking head
▪ Nodding	▪ Furrowing eyebrows
▪ Calm expression	▪ Tapping foot
▪ Sometimes putting a hand on the child's shoulder or arm affectionately	▪ Pointing at child
	▪ Rolling eyes
▪ Leaning forward	▪ Hands over mouth
	▪ Pacing
	▪ Crying

You won't realize you're doing these things unless you catch yourself in the moment—so next time you're listening to your child talk about something upsetting, mentally stop for a moment and "look" at yourself. If this were a movie with no sound, what would you see here? Does it look like you're angry, upset, impatient? Or calm and sympathetic?

Know the Goal

Make sure that you and your child are on the same page: The goal in any bullying scenario is not to "punish" the bully, but to end the problem.

The problem may end in a number of ways: Your child may learn enough resilience that the bully's words or actions don't matter anymore, the bully may move on to a new target, the bully may be removed from interactions with your child, the two of them may become best friends forever and go skipping through fields of daisies together . . .

As much as you may think that what you want right now is to see this rotten kid expelled from school and thrown onto an island for bad, bad children, that won't solve anything long-term if your kid hasn't learned anything from the experience. There will be another bully to take the first one's place. The world has no shortage of bullies, ready to pounce on a tempting target. The ultimate goal in these types of scenarios is to get your child out of crisis and out of physical and emotional danger. Leave the "punishment" to others.

Phase Two: Act on a Plan

Next we'll need to construct a plan that will see the child through the crisis period. A crisis period is defined by a period where one's coping resources have been exhausted and a person can no longer function the way he had before. This is a time that is most fraught with high emotion, fear, and hopelessness because there are no solutions in sight. It usually feels like nothing will work.

This crisis period, which usually lasts between one and fourteen days, is considered to have passed once the child feels able to reenter the routine of the precrisis life. The intensity and duration of the crisis period are determined by the amount of distress your child feels, which in some ways is a function of how you as a parent react. The crisis lasts until a plan can be found and acted upon.

There is no one-size-fits-all plan to stop bullying. It's more of a flowchart, where you first consider the simplest, most direct solutions—and if they don't work or aren't acceptable to the child, you move on to the more complex solutions.

Bully Stopper Guide:
Check-In Time

Once you've established that something has happened that sounds like bullying, it's time for the child to do a little assessment to figure out if the problem needs to be acted upon, and if so, how. The following are questions the child can ask herself while in the bullying situation, and afterward, when analyzing it:

1. Has this ever happened to me before?

One-time events don't always require action. Children often test out bullying behavior, without making a habit of it. If a child said something nasty, or shoved your child, took away a toy, etc., but that child had never done something like that before—or they were friends before—you might chalk it up to a bad day.

Children don't have great regulation over their emotions, and they sometimes change allegiances every five minutes. The person they were fighting with this morning might be their best friend this afternoon. If there's no immediate safety issue and no pattern of bullying established, lean toward a "wait and see" approach.

2. Does the bully know he hurt me?
Does he care?

We need to establish whether the other child is really bullying, testing out bullying, or not even aware of hurtful behaviors.

A boy named Jorge went to school with a boy named Owen all the way from first grade through high school. Jorge was a class comedian type, and Owen, who was overweight and a bit awkward, was often the butt of his jokes. But Jorge thought they were friends. He never actually meant to hurt Owen, and never realized that he was—he considered it friendly teasing. Owen had always laughed along with him.

It wasn't until the end of high school that Owen threw a fit.

"You've bullied me ever since we were kids! You ruined my life! I've had it with you!"

Jorge was stunned . . . and upset. If Owen had ever let him know that the teasing was hurtful and that he wasn't really "laughing along," Jorge would have stopped long before it became such a sore issue. He had empathy, and didn't mean to be a bully. Members of his family often teased each other in a playful way, lobbing insults at one another without actually meaning harm.

If the other child is aware that your child was hurt (emotionally or physically), how did he react? Did he apologize or try to help in any way? If so, that's also a sign of empathy and perhaps a sign that the child is simply "testing" bullying and is not truly a bully . . . yet.

3. Is there any way for me to laugh this off?

This is a hard one for a sensitive child to answer. Almost every time, the initial answer will be no. But the more the child can learn to smile, laugh, or grin along with the bullies rather than getting upset, the more likely it is that the bullies will give up trying to get a rise out of your child.

Try to work out a scale with your child, so he can check in with himself to determine how bad this particular event really is. On a scale from 1 to 10, where 10 is the worst, how embarrassing is this event? How hurtful is the comment? If it's below an 8, it can probably be laughed off, with some practice.

4. Am I in physical danger?

If the answer to this is yes, there can't be any "wait and see" time. Something will need to be done immediately, and it probably can't be done alone. But it still needs to be done with the child's understanding and consent—it's not in your best interest or the child's best interest to barrel through and take over the situation.

If the child is in a situation where he feels physically threatened, he needs to have "escape routes" and safety nets planned. Where will he go and who will he talk to? Can he walk into the guidance counselor's office, or the teachers' room, or the cafeteria? Can he go into the office and strike up a conversation with a school secretary, a cool teacher, or a coach? He doesn't need to talk to them *about the bullying situation.* He can come up with any excuse he likes—questions about homework, small talk about the weather . . . whatever he likes. It helps if the adult is aware that the child may do this and the reasons for it, but the child doesn't have to explain every time. You can even work out a code ahead of time with a "safe" office person, for example, and your child. Whenever your child comes in and talks about bad weather, the office person can take him in to a safer place.

5. Do I feel powerful enough to confront the bully myself?

If so, it's just a matter of formulating a time and place, and what words and body language to use. Maybe your child doesn't feel powerful enough to confront the bully in front of people, but if she could find a way to take the bully aside and talk to her privately, she'd be willing to try it. Maybe she could ask the girl to walk aside with her at recess, or she could approach the girl after class.

6. Can I rely on help from others?

Your child may have loyal friends who just don't know what's happening, or don't know how to help. They may need to hear specifically what to do: when your child needs someone to walk with, what words to say if your child is being picked on, when to get a teacher, and so on.

Maybe your child would feel strong enough to confront the bully if your child's friends were there for backup.

Using these questions, along with other tools, children can momentarily derail the momentum of playground or classroom events and create an opportunity to assess the danger they are in and decide on a strategy to help them handle the situation if it occurs again. These questions also help them distinguish between true bullying and one-time fights.

These guides also help children begin to think about the power of the bully in relation to themselves, and whether or not they can safely take action or count on others (friends or adults) to help them. Sometimes the solution is as simple as building the child's confidence enough to tell the bully, "Knock it off and leave me alone." It may be as simple as standing up straight, and giving the bully a look and a hand signal that says, *Hey, what's up with that?* Other times, the child will need more backup.

Overall, this plan builds on the first phase, using the information gathered during your conversations with your child to prepare and enact specific steps that will help resolve the immediate problem.

Role-Playing with the Child

It's important to go over likely scenarios with your child to help her rehearse what to say and do when the problem occurs.

Forget about insulting or threatening the bully.

Forget about telling your child to "just ignore it."

"Cute" and snappy comebacks are tough to pull off, but possible if your child feels comfortable with this strategy.

These examples are high-risk and likely to make your child look too affected by the bully's words or actions. Even "ignoring it" usually *is* a reaction. When a child is clearly pretending not to hear or see, it's a fun challenge for the bully to get louder and more abusive. It's funny to the bully that she's gotten to the target enough that she feels she *has* to pretend not to hear. And more often than not, the child is not a very good ignorer. There is usually plenty of body language to tell the bully that the bad behavior is working.

Therefore, what's more important is to instill a sense in the child that the bullying child's remarks and behaviors honestly don't matter . . . therefore, you don't need to pretend not to see or hear, you don't need to argue or cry; you can just give a little grin and reply, "Say whatever you like" and leave it at that, or even— gasp!—agree with the bully if the teasing isn't too bad.

Think of how many comedians America loves who rely on self-deprecating humor. Jay Leno doesn't get offended when people tell him he has a big chin. He agrees with them and even exaggerates it to make jokes about himself. Rodney Dangerfield made a career of insulting himself—probably playing off the comments children once made about him.

If your child is going to confront the bully, whatever your child chooses to say must be said as unemotionally as possible. Bullies absolutely love it when a child is frothing at the mouth, panting, crying, yelling, stomping away . . . that virtually ensures that the harassment will continue. Practice the tone of voice with your child. If your child has a favorite "cool" celebrity, it might help to pretend to be that celebrity when delivering the lines.

Work with your child on portraying confidence—standing straight, looking people in the eye, speaking calmly and firmly.

Here are some acceptable lines your child might use, depending on his level of comfort and resilience:

- Say whatever you like about me.

- Maybe you're right.

- Okay, whatever you say.

- Thanks!

If your child feels a little stronger and can use body language to stand up straight to bullies and look them in the eye, more assertive responses are possible:

- That's enough.

- I'm not interested in fighting.

- Please stop now.

- This isn't funny to me.

- Knock it off.

Tell your child *not* to use these words, which convey too much emotion or are too threatening and will probably produce the opposite of the desired result:

- Shut up.

- You're stupid.

- You're a jerk.

- That's not true!

- Am not.

- I'm telling.

- My big brother/father/neighbor/friend could beat you up.

- Liar!

- Get away from me.

- I hate you.

Don't Get Touchy-Feely

Sensitive kids expect other kids to be sensitive. When they're not, often the sensitive kid wants to tell the bully how she feels, particularly when they're young and the bullying is verbal. ("You hurt my feelings." "I don't like it when you say that!" "Stop, you're making me upset.") Some parents encourage this, too,

JORDAN'S STORY

Two older boys were bothering my son at school; they wouldn't let him pass in the hall. He was only six at the time. I told my son to take an alternate route or walk with a friend instead of being alone. I also told him to try to smile with the bullies and say "Peace be upon you" if he happened to encounter them again (we are Muslims, and that is the Muslim greeting). This is what he did, and it worked, perhaps because it was so unexpected.

believing that if the bully just understood that the words or behaviors were hurtful, they'd stop.

This is wishful thinking, and works only when you're not dealing with a true bully. True bullies don't have empathy—at least not for your child. They do not care that they've hurt your child's feelings . . . in fact, that's exactly what they want. So if your child expresses that his feelings are hurt, it's just as good as your child saying, "Way to go! You're accomplishing your goal. Please, keep it up! I might fall apart any second! Get popcorn!"

It's extremely hard for good people to believe that anyone could be so cruel at heart, especially children. We want to believe just talking to them and helping them understand the effects of their behavior can turn them all around. Some of them can and will learn empathy, sure. Others never will. But your child isn't there to be a teaching tool after the first time if he continues to be upset by bullying behavior.

This advice does not apply if your child is normally friends with the person who is now doing the bullying (or was once friends with the person): In that case, it may be that the friendship can be repaired and the bullying behaviors can stop if the children sit down and talk to each other about what's going on. But if you're dealing with a child who is a stranger to you, or someone who's never been nice to your child in the past, it's probably best that your child does *not* purposely let this bully know that her feelings are hurt.

Dealing with Relational Bullying

Dealing with gossip and rumors can be maddening, because kids want so badly to set the record straight and defend themselves against the allegations. But mostly, protesting backfires, and keeps the gossip alive.

So there's a very simple way for your child to react, consistently, when someone brings a rumor to her attention. Here it is:

GOSSIP HOUND: I heard you kissed that geek, Martin.
YOUR CHILD: Do you believe that I did that?

At this point, the gossip hound may say no. In that case, your child can answer, "Good. Then it doesn't matter." If the child says yes, or "I don't know," your child can say, "You can believe whatever you want. I don't care." Either way, that's as far as it should go. There should be no emotional protests to satisfy whoever started the rumor. Think about how powerful your child will feel when she can come back with something that may stop the negative comments.

Dealing with the silent treatment can be even more hurtful. A child who is shunned by her usual group—they stop talking to her, stop making eye contact, roll their eyes and whisper as she walks past, don't allow her to sit with them at lunch, etc.—can easily fall prey to depression.

In some cases, the friendships will be repaired, but if it happens more than once, it's probably not the best group for your child to depend on for social validation. Now, you may be thinking that these girls are everything to your daughter and that it is unrealistic for her to change this group. Well, is this your thinking or your daughter's thinking? Some children need to understand the value of friendship, openness to others, and diversity. Encourage your child to make friends in other groups, to approach people who aren't all part of the same clique. It's risky for a child to have friends from only one particular group—if all her friends are on the volleyball team, or they're all in chorus, or it's the same four or five girls hanging out every weekend, that's worrisome. There's too much riding on those friendships; if the most powerful girl in the group decides that your daughter is no longer "cool" or has done something she doesn't approve of, your daughter may feel completely adrift. The sooner your children understand that having friends in other places actually makes them feel stronger, you prevent the "all or nothing" response when something goes wrong in their social group.

Instead of spending her time trying to win her way back into her old group, or obsessing about those girls, encourage her to join a new after-school activity and talk to kids in other social circles. Or if they are dissing her one day, get her to react by role-playing the "I really don't care" attitude, which will bring the other kids back because they won't understand why your child doesn't care.

Phase Three: Preserve

Once the crisis is resolved, we move to the third stage, which I refer to as the preservation phase.

Understand that some kids will go through several crises before figuring out how to remain bullyproofed. So you'll have to repeat the process as it ebbs and flows.

The key to successful bullyproofing preservation is communication. I encourage parents to make in-depth discussions with their children a monthly routine, rather than a chance event. By talking regularly with your children about their social interactions and the bully dynamics they experience (which can change as your child changes), you'll develop a closer, more durable bond with your kids, and create natural opportunities for them to tell you when something is wrong. Once again, the adage "an ounce of prevention is worth a pound of cure" proves its worth.

However! (And this is a big "however!") There can be too much of a good thing. If the crisis has passed, *let it pass*. Don't ask about it every day. Don't insist on frequent reports from your child and the school if things seem to have returned to baseline. If your child comes home from school happy, let it go. Don't press and look for problems in every nook and cranny, or your child will learn to do the same thing: look for problems when there really aren't any.

If your child is a target, it's likely that he needs to learn how to care *less* about the bullies, not think about them more. Thinking about them all the time gives them more power over the child's life. So it's okay to check in once a week casually ("Is everything working with the plan we came up with?" "Are you having a better time in school this week?"), but there's no need to dig unless the child is continuing to give cues that something is wrong. Talking in-depth once a month is plenty during the preservation stages.

Working on Friendships

With the immediate crisis out of the way, the next step in order of importance is to build new friendships or strengthen existing ones. There is no better shield against bullying than peer friendships.

Misery Buddies

Often, kids who are bullied have just one or two close friends . . . who also tend to be bullied. Unfortunately, they can feed off each other's misery. They may be friends solely because of the shared experience of being mocked and tormented. They may get together explicitly to complain about the lousy kids they know and escape into their own world.

If you see this happening, do *not* attempt to separate the friendship. First, that's more likely to make the children feel even less understood and accepted, therefore wanting to cling to each other more tightly. Second, it can ruin your child's only buffer. Third, it can make your child less likely to ever reach out to other potential friends.

Instead, do everything in your power to help your child make other friends *in addition to* the one "misery buddy." And if you catch the misery buddies wallowing together, do what you can to get them involved in positive activities—taking them bowling or to a craft class, going to a park, baking a cake together, and so on. Try to help them develop a positive connection that isn't centered on the shared bullying experience, which can deepen their friendship.

Encourage Company

Ask your child what you can do to encourage her to invite kids to come over to the house to play. Make her feel that her room is "special," and that she has a couple of cool toys or games to play with, or activities that other kids would enjoy doing with her.

Although peers who are in the place where bullying takes place are the most "desirable" friends, any friendships at all are helpful. Maybe there's a cousin who your daughter sees only on holidays—

invite her to spend the weekend with you, or ask your daughter if she'd like to go there for a visit.

"You're the Same Age . . . Go Talk"

It's funny because we can probably remember hating it when our parents did this to us, if we think back hard enough, yet we still do it to our kids: assuming that they should be able to strike up conversation with anyone their "own age."

You're at a neighborhood party, and you see a boy who looks about your son's age, so you tell him, "He looks your age. Go talk to him."

To a child whose confidence is already ravaged by being on the receiving end of bullying abuse, "Go talk to him" sounds roughly like, "Go staple things to your forehead." Kids don't do well with "opening lines." They need activities to do together. Instead of sticking two kids together and saying, "Joe's mom tells me he likes soccer. You like soccer, too. Why don't you go talk to each other?" try involving the two of them in a game or project.

Put them in a situation where they'll need to work together— make them a team in a board game or charades, ask them to draw a birthday banner together, ask them to help you clear the table. If you know a new child is going to be visiting your house, prepare a fun activity—like a treasure hunt—that the kids can do together while the adults talk.

Gaining Social Confidence

True victory is achieved when the child feels friend-eligible and confident enough to know that no matter what a bully says, the child is still okay. Real self-esteem does not shatter when someone calls

WHERE TO FIND FRIENDS FOR YOUR CHILD

- Religious organizations
- Camp
- Athletic groups

- Dance class
- Volunteer activities
- Craft class
- Library groups

- Town youth centers
- Acting group
- Girl Scouts/ Boy Scouts

you "Big nose." Nobody likes being insulted, but it's much easier to get over it quickly if your self-esteem isn't in peril to begin with.

Your child develops social confidence by repeated small successes. If she learns that she can make kids laugh, or that she can make friends, that she's good at things (karate, music, gymnastics, etc.), that people have fun at her birthday parties . . . each of these things builds on the last.

Self-Defense Classes

Martial arts or other self-defense classes can go a long way toward building a child's confidence and even improving the child's body language, thereby making him look less like a target. A martial arts stance is a strong posture—it's the opposite of the hunched-over, head-down, insecure look many bullied kids sport all day long.

Jed is now a karate instructor in Ireland, but was once a bullied child. When he was in elementary school, he was pushed and shoved in the hallways between classes, punched and kicked by classmates, and teased for his lanky appearance and his name. He remembers one horrible time when kids in his class gathered in a huge circle and took turns punching and kicking him and calling him names.

He was also being physically and verbally abused at home, and his mother died when he was five years old. He believes that this caused him to be very withdrawn and an easy target. Things changed for him when he took up karate, though. At first, he took classes in secret, because he believed his father would punish him for learning to fight back. But when he was eleven, the family moved from England to Ireland, and he joined a karate club, where he won competitions. Not only did this give him a new sense of confidence, but it also got back to his new classmates—one of the kids in his class saw Jed compete, and word got around that this wasn't someone to mess with.

He finds this funny because he was even more ripe for bullying at the new school—not only was he the new guy, but he had an English accent in an Irish school, a quality that caused the kids to pick on the other English child in the class. But he was projecting a different image now. He felt stronger and better about himself.

Sometimes parents worry that martial arts classes will encourage their kids to become violent, become the aggressors. But this is generally not true at all. Most instructors emphatically teach that the skills are not to be used in anger or aggression, and are to be used only in the context of the class (or competition), or in self-defense when bodily harm is coming their way. The idea is to lessen the fear instilled by the bullies, not to become a thug.

My coauthor took jiu jitsu in her early high school years, and remembers that her sensei would say, "The best feeling is to walk away from a fight knowing what you could have done, but didn't have to." This is what real power is all about.

Is Fitting In Wimping Out?

One of the main reasons bullies pick on targets is that there's something unusual about the target—an out-of-style haircut, "geeky" clothes, a unibrow, thick glasses, and so on.

A young teenage girl was routinely teased because of her "mustache"—she had naturally dark hair on her upper lip. Hideous? No. But noticeable if you were up close. She wanted desperately to get rid of it, but her mother wouldn't allow her to go for waxing or use any other hair removal techniques. In her opinion, there was nothing "wrong" with this hair, the daughter was too young to worry about it, and the problem was with the other kids—not with her daughter.

Now, all of that might be true, ideally. Ideally, all of us would be comfortable in our own skin, understand that the snide remarks of others have no bearing on who we really are, and never worry about trivial things like a little facial hair. But in this case, the mother was putting too much responsibility on the young girl to be a "moral model." She was letting the girl walk around life with a "tease me" sign on her upper lip, when it was easily correctable.

As a result of her plummeting self-esteem, the girl became increasingly more withdrawn, never dated in high school, and became depressed. Was this worth it so the mother could prove her point? This was a caring mother who was trying to teach her daughter an important life lesson: Don't worry about what other people think of your appearance. But at some point, she should have realized that the lesson wasn't working, and it was time to do something to help relieve her daughter's pain.

Some kids have the inner fortitude to withstand teasing and still know that they're okay. If this teen had been a different sort of person, she might have been able to say to herself, "Okay, so I do have some facial hair. A lot of European women do. It doesn't make me ugly, and it's no big deal, so if they want to tease me, I don't care. It just shows that they're superficial people, not me."

Some kids can say this and mean it; others can say it, but not really convince themselves; others can have this attitude sometimes but lose it other times; and others can't even pretend to mean it.

When mental health professionals work with people with panic disorder, they often do it this way: They first give a medication to block the panic attacks, *then* they work on changing the person's thoughts, beliefs, and behaviors. It's often too difficult to make any real progress when the person is still dealing with severe panic attacks that could strike at any second, so the idea is to take away the immediate crisis, then work on the life changes that will make it less likely for the disorder to continue or come back.

This is similar to what I'm saying in this case. If your child is being teased about something that is changeable or preventable (clothing, buck teeth, hygiene, hairstyle, etc.), it's usually best for the child to change that item first, *then* work on building the child's resilience. A child who feels "cool" will have a much easier time acting "cool." A child who's consistently self-conscious and on the defensive, just waiting for that next hurtful remark, is going to have a much tougher time learning to hold his head high and be confident. And the more you point out the difference between what the child feels and what you think the child *should* feel, the more the child will feel like a failure.

It probably took you a long time to be secure in your values, the ones you now hold dear as an adult. Don't expect your children to walk into middle school with fully formed values and a solid understanding of who and what matters in life. If they need the stylish clothes and the hairspray and the contact lenses to feel okay about themselves for now, so be it. It's not about wimping out; it's about your child's emotional survival in some very difficult years, where fitting in (and therefore "blending" in) is of primary importance. It also helps kids feel that you listen, you care, and that you can relate, which are all important for a continuing positive relationship.

Approval of Peers

Sorry, Mom and Dad, but your words of praise just don't mean as much anymore as the child's peers' words do. As a child gets older, he begins to understand that the parent pretty much *has* to say nice things (you're biased!), and that what you say doesn't always match the way the rest of the world sees it. Children count on their peers to give them an honest appraisal of themselves.

You'll want to help the child cultivate skills that other kids think are special or cool. These can be major talents (like singing, playing a sport, etc.) or little, quirky things. A girl who was teased in the sixth grade learned to make "friendship bracelets," all the rage at the time. She would give them to kids she liked, and soon, she was taking "orders" for them, even from kids who teased her. Sometimes she worked on them during lunch or recess, but she usually made them at home. Another boy was a very good cartoonist, and he doodled a funny caricature of the teacher one day. A kid sitting next to him noticed it and told him to pass it around at lunchtime. Soon, he was drawing caricatures of anyone who asked for one. Again, this gave him a "cool skill" and made him feel more popular.

Similarly, quirky little skills like juggling, hacky-sacking, or doing impressions can translate to positive attention among peers. And this positive attention, even for something seemingly small, can set the stage for better self-confidence.

How It Plays Out

The specifics of your approach and your plan will differ depending on the context of the bullying behavior. Most incidents occur in predictable places: primarily at school, camp, and sports activities. So let's first examine your role as a parent and what sorts of bullying lessons you're teaching your children, then we'll address the specifics of how to enact a bullyproofing plan based on where the bullying is taking place.

THREE

How Parents Can Break the **Bullying** Cycle

If you ask a room full of parents, probably not one of them will say, "Yes, we exhibit bullying behavior at home," or "We encourage our children to be victims." But we're all pretty sure that *other* parents do that.

What's interesting is that bullies and targets often grow up in the same sorts of households.

A Typical Bully-Target Household

Bullies and targets often grow up in families where one parent is an authoritarian, and the other is the permissive one. See if this fits your family:

- One parent almost always gets his or her way.

- Onc parent yeses the other to death because it's easier than arguing.

- One parent sets the rules and is rigid about them.

- One parent apologizes to others for the other one's behavior.

- One parent uses ultimatums or threats to get his or her way.

- One parent is prone to yelling at/insulting/complaining to cashiers, waiters and waitresses, and customer service people.

Even if not all of it fits, but some of it does, you may be demonstrating (without meaning to) the bullying dynamic to your children.

Four Styles of Parenting

Psychologist Diane Baumrind's research of parenting styles is well respected in the mental health field. She defines four types of parenting styles:

- **Authoritarian.** An authoritarian is someone who is not very big on showing feelings, rigid about rules, and wants to remain firmly in control of the kids' lives. Obedience is highly valued, and kids are not encouraged to participate in decision making.

- **Authoritative.** Authoritative parenting, on the other hand, is still structured, but allows children to be more assertive and express their individuality. Authoritative parents set clear rules, but encourage kids to be part of decision making, and they listen to children's feelings with the aim of encouraging and supporting the kids' needs. Authoritative parenting has been positively associated with a reduced likelihood of adolescent smoking,[14] reduced risk of risky sexual behavior, and other high-risk activities.[15] It's also been documented as the most effective parenting style in numerous measures of children's social competence.[16]

- **Indulgent/Passive.** Indulgent parenting is characterized by a lack of rules, a high level of independence for the children, and acceptance of nearly all behaviors. This is not due to a lack of attention, however—indulgent parents care about their kids, but they don't discipline them or want to "stifle" them.

- **Uninvolved.** Uninvolved parents neither expect much from nor give much to their children. Parents who are neglectful, inattentive, or emotionally absent fall into this category. Children reared by uninvolved parents tend to rate the lowest in studies measuring academic performance, social skills, and many other areas.

Improving Your Parenting Style

Ideally, you want to create a situation where both parents fit the authoritative style. If you recognize that this isn't the case in your family, do what you can to strive toward that goal.

Authoritarian types are generally reluctant to change. Some are better about hearing criticism than others; if your spouse is the authoritarian, try asking, "What kind of model do you want to be?" and see if you can have a productive talk. You may need to talk things through together with a counselor, who can offer a less biased view on your parental roles.

It's important not to argue about parenting styles in front of the kids and to present a united front. Negotiating about rules, punishments, privileges, and so on should be done between the parents privately, and it's okay to say to the child, "We need a few minutes alone to talk about this. We'll come back and let you know what we decide."

During this time, try to come up with solutions that set clear boundaries, without taking away the child's ability to have input in the decision. Even if you choose not to agree with the child's wishes, you should still acknowledge that you heard those wishes and considered them, then explain why you made the decision you did.

You can also develop special signals between the two of you to cue each other if someone is being too rigid or too passive. Some parents are great at communicating through secret looks. Others have cue words they use when they notice one parent is going overboard, being too permissive, or clearly not paying attention to the child.

If you can't get an authoritarian parent to change, make sure your child spends time with other role models to balance his view.

Indulgent parents may need to be reminded that rules aren't bad, nor do they indicate a lack of love or a lack of "coolness" on the part of the parent. It can be very confusing for a child when one parent sets rules and the other doesn't enforce them, or actively foils them. Parents need to come to agreements about how they will handle disciplinary situations, and not undermine each other once they've reached decisions.

Questions to Ask Yourself

When I give talks to parents about bullying, the first thing I do is hand out a questionnaire and ask them to fill it out. Here's what it looks like.

1. In the last 90 days, have you been a target of:

    a. Teasing   Yes _____   No _____

    b. Name-calling   Yes _____   No _____

    c. Verbal threats   Yes _____   No _____

    d. Gossiping or rumors   Yes _____   No _____

    e. Exclusion or cliques   Yes _____   No _____

    f. Embarrassment in front of others   Yes _____   No _____

    g. Rude or uncivil behavior   Yes _____   No _____

2. Did it occur:

    _____ in the workplace?   _____ in a restaurant?

    _____ at home?   _____ on the Internet?

    _____ while shopping?   _____ over clothes that you wore?

    _____ at a sports event?   _____ something else related to

    _____ in the car?   physical appearance?

3. Who did the bullying:

    _____ a boss?   _____ friend/acquaintance?

    _____ work colleague?   _____ spouse?

    _____ child?   _____ other (who) _____ ?

    _____ parent?

4. In the last 90 days, have you been an observer of:

    a. Teasing   Yes _____   No _____

    b. Name-calling   Yes _____   No _____

    c. Verbal threats   Yes _____   No _____

continues . . .

d. Gossiping or rumors   Yes ____   No ____

e. Exclusion or cliques   Yes ____   No ____

f. Embarrassment in front of others   Yes ____   No ____

g. Rude or uncivil behavior   Yes ____   No ____

5. Did it occur:

____ in the workplace?   ____ in a restaurant?

____ at home?   ____ on the Internet?

____ while shopping?   ____ over clothes that the target wore?

____ at a sports event?   ____ something else related to

____ in the car?   physical appearance?

6. Who did the bullying:

____ a boss?   ____ friend/acquaintance?

____ work colleague?   ____ spouse?

____ child?   ____ other (who) _____ ?

____ parent?

7. In the last 90 days, have you been a participant in:

a. Teasing   Yes ____   No ____

b. Name-calling   Yes ____   No ____

c. Verbal threats   Yes ____   No ____

d. Gossiping or rumors   Yes ____   No ____

e. Exclusion or cliques   Yes ____   No ____

f. Embarrassment in front of others   Yes ____   No ____

g. Rude or uncivil behavior   Yes ____   No ____

8. Did it occur:

    ____ in the workplace?   ____ in a restaurant?

    ____ at home?   ____ on the Internet?

    ____ while shopping?   ____ over clothes that the target wore?

    ____ at a sports event?   ____ something else related to

    ____ in the car?   physical appearance?

9. What role were you in when you did the bullying:

    ____ a boss?   ____ friend/acquaintance?

    ____ work colleague?   ____ spouse?

    ____ child?   ____ other (who) _____ ?

    ____ parent?

10. What stands out in your mind as the worst incident you have seen in the past 90 days?

   _____

   _____

11. What stands out as a particularly memorable "bullying event" from your childhood? Or adulthood?

   _____

   _____

What Your Questionnaire Answers Reveal

This self-evaluation is to help you think about the role bullying has in your own life as a target, participant, or observer—or all three. We rarely think about ourselves as having anything to do with bullying, especially as adults. We think it happens to someone else. But the reality is that we are all involved in the bullying problem to some degree, some of us more than others.

Look at how many positive responses you have to the *a* through *g* questions. If you think about these situations carefully, you'll be surprised by how often you deal with these issues. More important, though, is how often children are exposed to these behaviors not from their peer relationships, but from the adults in their lives who role-model these behaviors without thinking of them as bullying behaviors.

Children don't necessarily evaluate or differentiate when they see their parents engaging in gossip ("Did you hear that so-and-so's son got arrested? I always knew he was trouble . . ."), exclusionary behavior (leaving out a neighbor or cousin from a party), name-calling (even privately, it's never okay to use racist, sexist, homophobic, or similar hateful remarks; children pick up on this remarkably well), or bullying that takes the form of yelling at a customer service person or telemarketer. All they see is that their parents do it, so it must be acceptable for them to do it. Whereas parents may do it only privately, kids will take it to school, camp, sports, and elsewhere.

We tend to think of bullying as a childhood problem only, but it definitely isn't. Maybe we stop naming it properly, but adults instigate and experience bullying frequently. The questionnaire is often an eye-opener for parents, who tell me they didn't realize how much bullying they still see as and participate in as adults. The coworker gossip can feel just as exclusionary as the gossip in the middle school cafeteria; the nasty boss can make you feel as lousy as the schoolyard bully did. And the bystander instinct doesn't change much either: We may witness bullying as adults and do very little about it because we don't want to become the next target.

That was a tense spot for several of us in line at a coffee shop recently, when a man insulted and screamed at the young lady behind the counter until she was in tears. It was ridiculous. It was bullying. And it would have been downright dangerous for any of us to try to stop him at that moment. My mind raced—"What do I do?" Someone called over a manager, who asked the man to leave, and as soon as he left, the rest of us in line comforted the young lady, telling her that she handled herself beautifully and that the man was way out of line.

That's the best you can do sometimes—the goal isn't always to be a hero and jump in front of bullets to save strangers. None of us knew if that man was on drugs, or carrying a weapon, and as much as we all wanted to get that poor woman out of his path of fury, we were too afraid of riling him up further and having him turn on us. So the goal was to minimize the damage afterward, showing the young woman that we all knew his actions were uncalled for and making sure that she was okay; letting her know that even though she felt isolated while that was going on, we were all on her side. This is an awful lot like what our children need from their peers, too.

Some of the worst bullies of our youth have ended up in jail or in minimum-wage jobs . . . while others are now the heads of giant corporations. Did they suddenly grow empathy after school ended? Probably not.

So it's a good idea to think about our own bullying experiences, both from our youth and in the present day, to give ourselves a point of comparison.

One of the most important things to note is what role we play in our adult lives: Are you usually the target, the bully, or the bystander? Take a look at which area(s) you checked in the questionnaire and see if you spot a trend. If you're playing the target role in adulthood, it's not surprising that your child is, too. Maybe the two of you will learn to break free from that role together!

If you or your spouse plays the bully role, that's equally problematic. Parents who bully—even without meaning to—tend to have children who either bully or become targets.

Using the Questionnaire to Raise Your Self-Awareness

One of the most helpful things you can do is to think about the questionnaire over the course of a week or so, to keep checking in with yourself to see if your answers were accurate. It's amazing how often you can catch yourself in the act once you become conscious of what you're looking for. Next time you're on the phone with your sister or your best friend and your child is in the room, monitor yourself . . . Are you speaking negatively about other people? When you complain about people at work, do you name-call or use nasty nicknames? Do you ever bully your spouse into doing something, or let your spouse bully you?

If you catch yourself in the act, the best thing you can possibly do—and it's powerful—is to admit you were wrong, and to tell your child that you messed up.

"You know, I shouldn't have said that," you might say. "I was gossiping just then, and that's not something I approve of. Sometimes I have to remember to tell people that I'm not comfortable talking behind other people's backs. I wouldn't want people to gossip about me. How about you?"

All children are going to mess up from time to time, just as adults will. By admitting you're fallible, too, you can teach your child a valuable lesson: that the important thing isn't being "perfect" all the time, but admitting mistakes and learning from them. That also encourages your children to be honest with you when they make mistakes. If you don't admit your faults, your children are less likely to take responsibility for their behaviors.

How to Make Your Child
Feel Powerless

If you really want to make your child feel small and powerless, use phrases like the following:

- Don't cry or I'll give you something to cry about.

- My way or the highway.

- Do that one more time, and I'll humiliate you in front of your friends.

- I don't care what you want; I'm the parent.

- If you do that again, I'll kill you.

- I brought you into this world and I can take you out of it.

- Do what I tell you or else!

- Keep it up, and I'll send you away.

- If you don't listen, you'll be grounded forever.

- Just wait until your father (mother) comes home.

- You don't deserve to be part of this family.

There are plenty of "threats" parents use without even thinking about it, because they obviously don't mean what they've said. When most parents say, "I'm gonna kill you!" of course they don't actually mean they're going to murder their children. But the children see and hear the anger and the threat anyway, and have learned that threatening others means you're powerful and the other person had better do what you say.

Whether children become bullies or targets largely depends on which parent they identify with. Either they'll see the power and decide they want it—so they adopt bullying behavior with their peers—or they sympathize with the other parent and copy the "weak" mannerisms, thus making themselves likelier targets.

Name-Calling

In my practice, I've been amazed by the array of insults loving parents will hurl at their kids when the parents get mad. I've heard parents call their kids "stupid," "idiot," "jerk," "baby," and plenty of other invectives. Do the parents actually mean it? No—they're angry about something, and that's how they let their kids know they're angry. It's a lousy way to do it, though, because there's already an uneven power balance in the inherent nature of the parent-child relationship. Name-calling makes a child see you as a bully. Try to become aware of the words you're using when you're angry.

Then there's the way to really ensure your child won't open up to you anymore: Use the bullying events against him. That is, when the child is getting on your nerves, say something like, "No wonder you're getting bullied! Look how annoying you're being!" or "If you're this much of a crybaby at school, I can see why you're getting picked on." There's a compassionate way to discuss the things the child is doing that may encourage bullies, and there's a finger-pointing, blaming way that just makes the child feel more out of control. If you want your child to trust you, you can't use the admissions he makes to you against him later.

Gossip, Gossip, Gossip

When I talk to parents, this part of my questioning often surprises them—and opens their eyes. How much do you gossip?

Most people think they're not into gossiping, but if you really take time to examine your own behavior, you may surprise yourself. Do you talk to your sister on the phone and tell her about Aunt Kristina's divorce? Do you talk to your neighbor about other neighbors? Do you tell your mom about the stupid things your in-laws do, or your husband about your coworker who you wish would get fired?

We all do, to some degree. It's part of normal conversation. And what we're really teaching our kids when we do it is that it's perfectly okay to say nasty things behind people's backs. Young kids can't differentiate and understand that you're not supposed to say certain things in front of people—hence the ever-embarrassing moments when a child blurts out something to a dinner guest that you said earlier.

In my neighborhood, one kid told another, "My dad says that your dad is a schmuck," and we all tried to figure out for the next ten minutes or so what the word "schmuck" meant—until the second kid told his dad what had been said about him and asked for an explanation of the word.

Their hurtful "teasing" may actually be an emulation of the kind of gossip they see you do. If you regale your husband with a story of how stupid that cashier was today, don't be shocked when your child begins calling kids "stupid," and believing that kids who aren't as smart as other kids deserve to be put down. Young children who know curse words and use them when speaking about others have learned them from places outside of their children's books, so be aware: they are probably learning those words from home.

When I visited a friend a few months ago, she stopped to take a phone call. It sounded like she was talking to a dear family member. "How are you? It's great to hear from you!" All sweetness and light. The moment she hung up the phone, in front of her daughter and me and everyone else in the room, she said, "I can't stand that bitch."

What lesson has she just imparted on her daughter? It's okay to be two-faced.

As children move into the preadolescent and adolescent years, they'll take gossip to a whole new level. It's very difficult to teach kids (girls, in particular) not to gossip when they hear their parents gossip about family members, friends, and neighbors. Parents usually don't think of what they're doing as gossip, but the moment you begin saying something about a person that you wouldn't want that person to hear, it's probably gossip. This includes the "So how long do you think it'll last?" comments at a person's wedding, the "How did so-and-so get a promotion?" comments at work, and so on.

Become aware of how often you participate in discussions like this, and how often your children are within earshot. This is a constant challenge in our own lives when we speak about others and end up putting out information that may have been said behind their backs, even if it was not to hurt their feelings.

Girls, especially, are conditioned early not to speak directly. They're taught to be good and sweet, stifle confrontational feelings, and mask their aggression, so starting as early as age three, they often show signs of relational bullying. It's socially more "feminine" for them to ignore and whisper and roll their eyes, rather than actually approach someone and talk out a problem. Be mindful of this tendency and make sure you're teaching your children about healthy communication. The question is, are you using healthy communication in your own relationships?

Healthy communication has to do with teaching your kids how to be direct with each other. Try to role-model this in your own life with those adults that you feel you need to be clear or direct with. Use yourself as a learning tool for your girls. Encouraging girls to speak directly to each other when their feelings are hurt will teach

PROMOTE POSITIVE GOSSIP

Encourage your children to start "positive gossip." Instead of saying negative things behind others' backs, they can have fun spreading positive rumors instead. Positive rumors are things like, "Can you believe what a good friend she is?" or "She's someone everyone can count on because she always comes through," or "He's someone you can trust with your problems because he'd never embarrass you in front of others."

It can be difficult for a child to say, "I don't want to participate in your negative gossip" when a friend or acquaintance starts in on someone. Silence may be an easier response, and it's still effective; if you don't join in with the gossip, people generally get the idea that you don't approve of it. Then the child can get the message across by finding excuses to promote positive gossip—any excuse will do, from "I really like her clothes" to "I bet he'll be a famous musician one day." The goal is just that if you're going to talk behind someone's back, make it about something nice.

them a very valuable skill. For example, if you find out a friend has gossiped about you, think about calling her and telling her that you heard that she had said something about you behind your back. Tell her what you heard and tell her that this hurt your feelings. Only then can you begin to role-model the appropriate kinds of open and direct communication with your daughter.

If you see that your daughter is saying mean or hurtful things about another girl, jump on it. Tell her that she said some things that sounded pretty nasty, and that if those things were said about you, it would hurt. If you pay attention to the meanness or nastiness you see in yourself or your kids' words, you can begin to change the bullying behavior that harms relationships.

Use this time to share your own stories with your children about gossip and rumors, and how this may have hurt you, or how you hurt someone else. The personal stories coming from a parent mean so much more because they see you as real, and this allows you to bond more closely when these situations arise. And believe me, because gossiping is so common among adults, it is commonplace among kids.

Lessons at Starbucks

So there I was at my local coffee spot, in the midst of a long discussion with a colleague of mine about a bullying presentation. A woman at the next table overheard our conversation, and she interrupted to say, "Can I ask you a question?"

"Of course," I said, and she told me that she was having a problem with her daughter. The daughter had earned a reputation as a gossip, and her friends didn't want to talk to her anymore. For almost half an hour, I spoke with her about gossip and made suggestions about what her daughter could do to either make some new friends or try to salvage some of her old friendships. We talked about girls being indirect with each other, and how it is easier for them to avoid feelings of competition, jealousy, anger, and unfairness.

Then the woman thanked me as she saw that her friends had arrived. She walked over to the group of women . . . and immediately began gossiping about a neighbor. "Can you believe that she did that today? I can't believe anyone likes her . . ."

I was floored. It was so comical that I almost couldn't believe what I was witnessing. There was a total disconnect—the woman had been listening intently to what I told her, but she was hearing it strictly on an intellectual level. She made no emotional connection to what I was saying; she didn't relate it to her own life at all.

This put me in a strange predicament. I didn't know whether to just let it go or say something to her. What would you have done?

I thought it through and realized that this was a perfect

bystander situation, and I was going to have to practice what I preached. In my role as bystander, I could have let her continue gossiping, or I could have tried to do something about the situation. Knowing that she came to me for advice about her daughter, it would have been wrong for me to let this go without pointing out how her own behaviors might influence her daughter—so that's what I did.

I could have embarrassed her in front of the other women, but that would have been wrong. Instead, I tapped her on the shoulder and asked if I could speak with her for a moment. When we had stepped away from the group, I told her what I had just observed. "I have to tell you something. We just spent a lot of time talking about your daughter's gossiping. I don't know if you're aware of this, but as soon as your friends got here, you immediately began gossiping about a neighbor."

Her face turned bright red. She just muttered, "Okay, thank you," and walked away. For all I know, she may have begun gossiping about me as soon as I walked out. But I knew from her embarrassed reaction that I'd at least made the connection for her—she'd recognized that I was telling the truth. What she chose to do with the information from there was not in my control, but it sure helped me to understand where her daughter had learned that this behavior was acceptable.

Disciplining without Bullying

Because of the innate power imbalance between parent and child, it can feel like any form of discipline must be bullying—how do you tell a child what to do and what not to do without being a bully?

Disciplining is about structure. Kids need to know the boundaries of what behaviors are acceptable and what behaviors aren't.

Sit down with your kids when they get to elementary school age and talk to them about what are acceptable behaviors in the house, what are acceptable behaviors out of the house, and what are unacceptable behaviors in and out of the house. Don't assume that the child innately understands, for example, that it's okay to jump around on your couch, but it's not okay to jump around on someone else's couch. Have these discussions again when the rules need to be revised as kids get older.

Consistency is important. Show your kids that you're serious about the rules of the house, and not just that you'll enforce them randomly when you're in a bad mood. Be clear and spell out how you feel about things like swear words (Is "damn" okay?), fighting, curfews, dating, how to treat teachers, and so on.

In school, kids have to live by a set of rules. They know what's expected of them and what the consequences are if they're late to class, skip class, talk back to a teacher, don't do their homework, and so on. They know they're going to lose ten points on their grade if the term paper is a day late. They know they'll get detention for being late to homeroom. House rules that are meaningful to your family can be just as straightforward. Kids need this structure as a way to help them learn about boundaries, and what is right and wrong. Teaching them to follow rules helps them feel that they are part of a community that works together. If they are allowed to make up their own rules, or see that you are not consistent with them, how will they learn to live with others, be respectful of them, and trust that there is some purpose to rules that we all live by?

With young kids, you'll have to formulate the consequences of bad behavior. It's best to give them an idea up front of what the consequences are if they break rules. But once kids get a little older—to their preteen years—they can formulate consequences with you. A conversation might go like this:

"You know that we feel strongly about cursing, and that's important to our family. So if you curse at your sister, what do you think would be a fair consequence?" Then you negotiate with them. You can go down the whole list of potentially unacceptable behaviors and formulate appropriate consequences together. And then when it happens, the punishment is not made in anger. They understand that they crossed the line, and made the choice to break a rule. They're involved in the process—they feel some ownership of it, which helps them learn about self-regulation. I know this sounds different from the rules we were taught by our parents, that we never questioned. Kids, though, especially teens, will have more ownership of their behavior if they feel that they are not being preached to; they want you to respect them by showing respect.

Then there's the positive side of discipline: As kids get older, what they want most is to earn more freedom for themselves. So based on how well they stay within the rules, make sure you're giving them opportunities to earn more freedom. Holding the lines really rigidly ignores what kids need. As they get older, they can take on more responsibility for their behaviors and they'll need parents to be flexible and shift the system to accommodate their changing responsibilities and needs. The rule about always coming straight home from school and doing homework before being allowed to "play"—does a ninth grader really need that heavy-handed structure, or can she be trusted to come up with her own homework schedule? Let her earn that right by showing that she (almost) always finishes her homework on time. If she can't, then more structure and order can be added on until she proves that it can be managed. Put the responsibility on the kids!

The more you can do to remove emotion from discipline, the better you are. Consequences should not be decided in the moment when you're angry. As much as possible, they should be spelled out

BUT WHAT ABOUT TEMPER TANTRUMS?

It can be tremendously difficult to keep your cool when your child is having a temper tantrum. How do you inform him that his behavior is unacceptable without yelling, when you can't even get a word in?

Let the kid tantrum out until he calms down, and walk out of the room if you want to.

"Until your behavior stops, I'm not going to be here to witness it. I'm leaving."

Go to the bathroom, lock the door, and wait a little while. Your child can't listen effectively when he's in the middle of a tantrum, and you can't discipline effectively when you have to yell over him. Don't get into a shouting match. Just wait him out.

in advance. If it's too late for that, just remember to take control of yourself, breathe, and take a break before deciding on punishment. You can take a break for a couple of hours, if needed, to wind down and be rational. When you're emotional, there's a greater chance you'll cross the line and frighten your child with your voice or words. If your intention is to make her feel worthless, you're abusing your power.

It veers into the bullying realm when your emotion gets the best of you and the punishment is greater than the crime. That sets up a bad situation where the child fears you, and shuts down communication. Your goal is not to have your child distrust you and close you off, but there won't be an opening until you are emotionally ready to show him that you are back in control of yourself.

If one spouse tends to blow up in anger and the other doesn't, consider coming up with a sign between the two of you—a code word or signal that means, "You're going too far. Cool down."

Children do not open up to parents they fear. If you want to be informed when a child is in danger, or being tormented by bullies, or has witnessed a terrible bullying incident, you can't let the child feel like your behavior is just like the bully's.

Your Children Aren't Perfect, and It's Okay for Them to Know It

A parent's natural instinct is to deny, deny, deny anything the tormentors say, and teach their kids that they're gorgeous, brilliant, talented, perfect little people. And when the children are very young, they buy into it—they agree that they're perfect. Soon, though, the other kids knock them off their perfect pegs and begin pointing out all their flaws. Sometimes the kids are just being obnoxious and making up things because your child is giving them the emotional reaction they want, and sometimes there's some truth to what they say.

Maybe your kid is teased for being a nerd, or having a big nose. And you know what? Maybe your kid *is* a little nerdy and does have a big nose. Rather than pretending that the opposite is true and acting horrified that these cruel children are spreading such terrible lies, use this as an opportunity to say, "So what?" Tell them about famous people who were once called geeks and nerds when they were young—people like Jennifer Garner and Sarah Michelle Gellar. Point out the child's more attractive features.

A child who is taught to believe that she's perfect is going to have a harder time accepting it when that bubble gets burst than a child who has a more realistic self-image. Make sure your kids understand that everyone has little things about themselves that they wish were different, or that they don't like very much, but that usually they realize that those things aren't very important. Sometimes they even learn to like the things that make them feel different and weird when they're young. This is what resilience is all about.

Denying a quality that your child actually *does* have makes that quality seem really bad. "Oh, my goodness! You're not a nerd! Those kids are crazy!" Now the kid knows that you think nerds are bad, and that it's an insult to be called that. But is it really so bad to have a little "nerd pride"? It may be best to teach your child how to be a little self-deprecating and make fun of himself, which takes the sting out of those words when other people say them.

Do You Tease at Home?

Wait, before you look guilty: That's a good thing! Playful teasing is a healthy, positive thing. It teaches your kids not to take themselves too seriously, and not to get terribly offended by every little comment. I can remember at our own dinner table, letting my kids make fun of my imperfections in a relaxed, fun way. It really creates ease. It provides an opportunity for us to laugh with each other, which is very different than laughing at each other. Feeling safe and acknowledging imperfections allows us to develop a more realistic self-image.

You may be able to gauge how your child reacts to peer teasing by watching how he reacts when you tease. If he whines or yells or cries, you know you'll need to work on his oversensitivity. Talk to him about the difference between hurtful teasing and just playing around. Tell him that teasing can be a sign of affection, and that people who really like each other can joke with each other without trying to be hurtful. Then use an example, and make fun of yourself. Show your child that you are okay being imperfect.

But be aware of how others in the family react, too—does Mom pout every time Dad makes a joke about her bad cooking? Does big sister get upset when Mom makes a dig about how long she spends fixing her hair? If you're trying to teach a child not to react so strongly to teasing, make sure the other family members are role-modeling the right behavior. It's a positive atmosphere when family members can tease each other back and forth without any real hurt or resentment.

Downplaying and Overplaying

Let's say your child has come to you with complaints about other kids who are picking on her. After a while of listening, you determine that your child is not in any real danger and the incidents don't seem too terrible. But your child is stuck on repeat, unloading all the injustices and slights and behaviors she didn't like that day.

One of the things our children are looking for from us is a cue about how to react. In part, they learn how seriously to take things based on how seriously *we* take things. So if the bullying incidents are not awful, it's important that you don't let your child focus on them more than she already is.

A friend of mine tells a story of a boy who's now in high school whose mother made such a practice of "overempathizing" with his every complaint that he's a walking excuse. He can't play in gym class today because he got a paper cut. He can't go to school because he stubbed his toe. He should be excused from the test because he forgot his locker combination, so he couldn't take his books home. He can't practice piano because he ate too many Cheez Doodles.

The problem is that his mother made such a huge deal of all these types of ailments and problems that he believed they were all legitimate and worthy of worry. Not surprisingly, he is teased a great deal in school and has few friends. His mother is wildly upset about that, too.

She taught him to be helpless and victimized, though. She taught him that every small problem was a big problem, and that he should be exempt from any sort of discomfort in life. Of course she meant well: She wanted him to have a perfect, happy life, and she never wanted him to feel pressured in any way. But now he's heading off to college in a few months and is still under the impression that the world should stop every time things don't go perfectly for him.

He's a walking target for bullies, even at an age where bullying has diminished. And he makes a big deal of every perceived insult. This isn't surprising, given that he learned that his mother would freak out whenever he related stories of normal childhood conversations. She would have done much better by him to have helped him put things in perspective. Not every incident of teasing is emotionally devastating, unless you choose for it to be. But when children sniff out someone who's going to be a "baby" about every little comment, the ones prone to bullying are going to tear him apart, even if they wouldn't have noticed him otherwise.

Why Some Fat Kids Are Popular

Lots of people think their kids are bullied because of a specific, usually physical, thing—that the child is overweight, wears glasses, has braces, is too skinny, etc. While it's true that any of those things can make a child more vulnerable to being teased, it's almost never the whole story. Otherwise, how would you explain the popular kids who don't look like little Calvin Klein models?

There are some kids who just transcend their teasable qualities. A colleague of mine remembers a boy in her high school who was pretty obviously gay—he was a ballet dancer, and in the school choir, and his speech and mannerisms were effeminate. Almost certainly, somewhere along the line, other boys called this kid "fag" or insulted him for his (apparent) homosexuality. But you wouldn't know that, because by high school, he was so secure in who he was and so self-confident that he was well liked by just about everyone, including the "cool" kids.

The jocks didn't hang out with him, but they didn't bother trying to make fun of him either—what good would it do? He was a happy guy with a good sense of humor and plenty of friends. He wasn't the type who looked like he might have a breakdown any second, so he was no use to bullies. They're not interested in picking on people who seem well adjusted. They want the kids on the edge.

This guy "came out" after high school, to no one's great surprise. Soon thereafter, he would joke around about it. "I bought a pair of leather pants. I know—I'm such a fag!" And that's what made him bullyproof—it just wasn't going to bother him if kids had tried to take advantage of his "vulnerability." He knew his sexuality was different from the norm, he knew he was effeminate, and he didn't care. His parents helped him feel acceptable as he was, and he internalized their belief that he really was okay.

Then you have kids who are obese, or in wheelchairs, or who have speech impediments, who manage to navigate through youth with seeming social ease because they just don't let those teasable spots be a big deal. Instead of pouting or acting indignant when someone says he's fat, the resilient kid will say with a grin, "Yep, I'm fat. So what?"

The Power Contest: Keep the Pins Standing

I'm going to tell you the most important concept you can teach your child if he is being bullied. Bullying is a contest with a predictable course. The contest is: The person who looks cooler in the end wins. What does the person win? Power.

The bully starts with the upper hand because he's taking the first shot, and purposely trying to catch the target off-guard.

So here the two are, bully and target, in a big bowling tournament.

(Bowling tournament? Yes, that's what I said. Go with me for a minute!)

It's not a normal game, though. The bowler isn't competing against another bowler. He's competing against the pins. The bully is the bowler, and the target's reactions are the pins.

The bully winds up, and hurls his ball down the lane. He wants that strike. How will he know if he got a strike? Because his target will react strongly. His point system will go something like this: If the target . . .

Frowns: 1 pin

Rolls eyes: 2 pins

Folds arms: 3 pins

Does a bad job of pretending not to hear: 3 pins

Makes a face: 4 pins

Gets flustered: 4 pins

Groans or sighs: 5 pins

Tries to come up with a zinger of a retort, but fails: 6 pins

Yells: 6 pins

Runs away: 7 pins

Tattles: 8 pins

Puts his hands over his ears: 9 pins

Trips, spills food, or other clumsy act: 9 pins

Cries, gets angry, becomes emotionally out of control: Strike!

Of course, the target is likely to do more than one of these things at once—groaning and folding his arms, maybe—so you have to add up the points from each act. Anything ten or above is a strike. Anything less than that, but more than zero, is encouraging the bully to try for a spare.

But now you may be wondering: How can the pins ever win the bowling tournament?

Well, in this particular kind of contest, the winner is whoever looks cooler at the end, right? If the bowler gets an impressive score at the end—lots of strikes, some spares—then the bowler looks cooler. People want to high-five him. He made a mockery of those pins.

But if he gets an embarrassingly low score, he looks pretty uncool, because he couldn't knock down those pins. They're still standing, and he has to walk off in shame. The pins look cooler. The target wins.

To achieve this, the pins need to stand strong and tall, and be really hard to knock down. The pins get a little stronger when the child shows these reactions:

- Smiles in the face of adversity

- Laughs off criticism

- Makes a new friend

- Stands up for himself without whining, yelling, crying, or trying to insult the bully back

- Tells the bully that he can say whatever he wants, it doesn't matter

- Shows no emotional or behavioral reaction to bullying

"Shows no emotion" doesn't mean "feels no emotion," of course. Behavioral success means that the child can sit up tall with a smile on his face, even while being teased, and keep his eyes on the bully. The child may have to learn how to exercise a great deal of restraint not to allow his anger or fear or sadness to show. But the good news is that he shouldn't have to fake it for very long; once a bully has figured out that a particular target is no longer easy to knock down, he'll give up. It'll take a few tests, surely—especially if that target was a really easy one before. Bullies don't like to walk away from the bowling lanes where they made so many strikes before. It can take some convincing to show the bullies that the pins are now nailed into the lane and just aren't going to fall over, no matter what.

But there's an old saying that goes, "Fake it till you make it." Yes, it'll seem like a difficult job to keep those pins standing the first few times the ball comes hurtling down the alley. But a funny thing happens in most cases: not only does the bowler give up when he realizes he's losing the tournament, but the pins stop fearing him so much, too.

Bullied kids are "supposed" to be the ones that look stupid at the end of a bullying incident. They're "supposed" to be the ones freaking out and upset. But the funny thing is that this role can reverse if the target can learn to show that she really does not care what the bully thinks.

In the target's mind, there needs to be a shift. "Who the heck are *you* to make fun of me?" If that shift can be achieved, the contest can turn around and the target can have the upper hand. The bowler will have to overextend himself to try for the strike, and just wind up with gutter balls, and get frustrated.

So teach your kids about this contest.

Teach them that it isn't personal—it's about winning. Bullies say whatever they can to whomever they can to rack up the score. If it isn't you, it will be someone else, so don't play the game with them. Your power is in your ability to frustrate their game. The

SHERRYL CLARK'S STORY

When my daughter was about ten years old, our next-door neighbor's son, a twelve-year-old boy, starting hassling her at school. He began by pushing her, and then he started spitting on her. She was way too small to fight back, and didn't want me to tell the teachers. So I put my thinking cap on. I came up with this solution. I told her, "Next time he spits on you, give him a really big smile and say cheerfully, *'Thank you.'*" She thought I was crazy but decided to give it a try. After doing this twice to him, he stopped bullying her altogether!

Neither she nor I could believe it had worked so fast, but it did. I can't guarantee it would work in every situation but I was glad it did this time.

bullies want to rack up more bowling trophies, so they're just looking for wobbly pins. Teach your kids how to win by just standing tall and not giving up their pins by showing reactions. You might try asking them to literally keep score in their minds—count up the pins they lost at the end of a bullying incident and see where they need to improve to get better at this contest. If they didn't lose any, then the bully got a gutter ball.

If the target can stay cool, the target wins power.

Your child needs to stop accepting defeat and tell herself, "I could win this thing." This contest may require some training and practice, but it's one that's well worth winning!

Validating Their Feelings

One of the challenges of teaching your kids how to have a thicker skin is not to minimize their feelings in the process.

Of course bullying hurts. And your child shouldn't have to lie and say it doesn't . . . but that's not what this is really about. It's about winning a contest. Pretending that bullying doesn't hurt is just a skill to use to be a better competitor in this particular contest. It's still fine to let out one's true feelings with "safe" people—friends and family who will listen. However, I can tell you that, with practice, your targeted kids can feel like the real winners, and it doesn't take long to happen.

In the process of listening, you need to convey two things: "I sympathize with you" and "Now let's figure out what we should do about this." It's too easy for a child to get stuck on the first part—the "Ouch, it hurt; he's so mean" part, which probably needs to come out, but won't get the problem resolved. Part of your job is to keep the conversation moving along.

One way to do that is to ask the child to work on putting things in perspective. "How bad was it?" "How bad did that make you feel?" "Did you feel very upset when that happened?" If it's not too extreme, then try to redirect the conversation: "Okay, is there anything we can do about this today or tomorrow?" "What will you do if it happens again?" Then try to change the subject to something positive. If it is something extreme, it'll require more extensive conversation. But still, try to keep moving the conversation toward plans of action instead of wallowing in hurt, embarrassment, and anger. Tell your child to keep focused on the score: the more gutter balls for the bullies, the higher your score and the more fun you'll have in this game.

Teaching Friendship Skills

As parents, we can get a bit overwhelming when we want our kids to meet new friends. When I was a kid, my dad would try to be helpful but end up humiliating me. We'd go on vacation, and the first day, he was on a mission to *make* me connect and meet other kids. At the pool, he'd walk over to a boy and say, "This is my son, Joel. What's your name?" And the boy would say his name . . . and my dad would walk away and leave me there.

I felt like such a reject! I wanted to die.

I didn't realize how many other parents did similar things. A friend tells me that her mother would often say, "Those girls look about your age. Go talk to them." If she didn't, the mother would walk over and try to play "friend matchmaker," which made the girl feel ridiculous. It sent the message to the other girls that this girl was so pathetic that her mom had to find friends for her. And what if they had nothing in common? How awkward to stand there trying to find things to talk about and realize that they're completely incompatible.

One time, the mother even did this with a couple of girls who didn't speak English! The mother heard two little sisters speaking French while building a sandcastle on the beach, and thought they were cute, so she marched over to them with her daughter in tow and used gestures to ask if they'd play with her daughter. They seemed to say yes, though with some confusion . . . and the girl spent the next hour trying to figure out how to get out of this silly situation with two sisters who weren't in the least bit interested in hanging out with a stranger they couldn't even communicate with.

Humiliating your kids into talking to people is usually going to backfire. Instead, do some role-playing at home. Except for very young kids, you don't need to teach them exactly what "lines" to use to introduce themselves and make conversation, but you can guide them about what sorts of topics they can bring up and how to find out if they have things in common—such as what sports they like, what television shows they watch, what singers they like, what computer games they are into, if they have brothers and sisters, and so on.

Social language changes every generation, so it's risky for a parent to try to coach too much. Mostly, what you want to convey to your kids is that they might have a lot of fun with other kids, that there's plenty about them that's going to be interesting to other kids, and that they can and will find friends if they're willing to open up a little.

Remember to role-model friendship skills, too. If your kids see that you have a great relationship with your own friends, they're more likely to pick up on good friendship skills. If they see that you avoid phone calls, groan whenever So-and-So says she's stopping by, or gossip about your friends, they're not going to understand what's so great about having friends, or how to treat friends properly.

A Visiting Bully

You may encounter a situation where bullying occurs in your home, among your child's friends or acquaintances. Often, this is two-against-one bullying, where three kids are playing together and two of them turn on the third.

When kids are under your watch, you need to enforce the rules that you feel are right for your family. It's your right and duty to tell kids when their behavior is unacceptable, even if their own parents don't comment on that same behavior. You're the surrogate parent during the play date.

A friend of mine has an interesting way of handling things when she sees a child being mean to someone else in her home: She tells the bullying child, "This kid is now under your watch. If anything else happens that's upsetting or makes him cry, you're responsible. Do everything you can do make him feel good, or you're the one who will go home." By doing this, she lets the bully know she's

FATHERS MATTER

Psychologists in Canada set out to find what parenting styles encourage kids to become empathetic adults. They determined that of all the factors studied, the most important predictor of empathy in children was the father's involvement in child care. The other important predictors were: "maternal tolerance of dependent behavior, maternal inhibition of child's aggression, and maternal satisfaction with the role of mother." [17]

watching, and that a lack of empathy will lead to negative consequences.

The risk to this is that some manipulative bullies will then take the target aside and threaten: "Don't you cry again or I'll get you back in school tomorrow!" So it's smart for parents to address this, too. "I will know if this kid feels upset, so don't talk to him and tell him not to react if something bad happens." You don't have to say how you'll know. You'll just know. Parents have magic!

Self-Assessment

It's not always easy to recognize and own up to the things we may do as parents to model bully behavior or target behavior. As you're reading these words, you may believe your parental role modeling is perfect. But keep an eye out over the next couple of weeks. Become more aware of what your child is seeing.

Certainly, not every bully or target becomes so because of bad parental role models. And the issue here isn't looking for a spot to place blame, but for things to improve to help the child figure out what to strive for. As a parent, you're a very important influence on the way the child figures out how to treat people, and how to react when others do things we wish they wouldn't.

Be conscious of your own interactions with others—everyone from your spouse to your in-laws, the wait staff at restaurants, bill collectors, your boss, and your neighbors. The way you talk to and about them in front of your kids matters. Let them see that you don't approve of bullying or gossip, and that you neither engage in it nor become a victim of it in your own life. Think about that questionnaire at the beginning of the chapter, do it again, and think about your roles as an adult: Are you a target, an observer, or a participant in the same behaviors that you want your children to manage? If you do see yourself involved, it's okay: Use this as an opportunity to try a little harder not to gossip or to be so aggressive yourself. Or try to speak up next time your feelings are hurt. When you do it a little better, and admit that you're not perfect, you're teaching your kids resilience once again. Good job!

FOUR

Bullying in School

READING, WRITING, AND RESILIENCE

Every school—from preschool to grad school—has bullies, targets, and bystanders. If a school official says, "We don't have that problem here," don't believe it. Some schools are much better at dealing with the problem than others, but wherever there are children, there is bullying.

Approximately 20 percent of children (with some research pointing to much higher figures) experience bullying that greatly interferes with their school experience.

Bullying can affect your child's ability to learn in many ways, some of which can be linked to the depression, anxiety, and emotional and mental distress that targets of bullies typically suffer. (School is challenging enough for most of our kids—just imagine trying to master algebra while simultaneously being belittled and victimized!)

Gary Won't Go Back to School

It was about nine thirty on a Sunday night when Linda called me. She wasn't someone I worked with regularly—the parent organization she belonged to had brought me in to speak a few months before—but nonetheless, the mixture of anger, fear, and anxiety in her voice would have been obvious even to a perfect stranger. She wanted to talk about her son, Gary.

An hour before, Gary had shocked the family by announcing: "I'm not going to school, tomorrow or ever again! Everyone hates me and teases me. They make fun of me on the bus and push me out of my seat, and take my hat and my books and throw them." Though Linda tried to listen to her son, she was soon overwhelmed by feelings of outrage and indignation. Who were these boys who dared terrorize her son? What were their names? Did she know their parents? She felt angry toward these kids because they had made her son feel bad.

But instead of reassuring him that his tormentors would be punished, Linda's outrage only seemed to upset Gary more, and crying inconsolably, he withdrew to his room, refusing to speak to her. Gary was already deeply shamed by his victimization, and was most likely upset by Linda's outburst because he felt that she was angry at him.

Feeling confused and alone, he withdrew further; when Linda tried to soothe him, he put the covers over his head and shut down. Linda couldn't get through to Gary on her own, and her husband was out of town and couldn't be reached. Desperate to alleviate her son's suffering and her own feelings of helplessness, Linda remembered hearing me speak a few months before, found my number, and called me.

Gary had been teased a few times in the past, but this year in the fifth grade, a group of boys had begun to terrorize him with increasing frequency and viciousness. He was often in the nurse's office with painful stomachaches. He missed more and more school owing to bouts of an unexplained illness, and had even started staying home on the weekends rather than going out to play with friends. Basically, Gary was protecting himself as best he could by removing himself from social situations where he felt anxious or unsafe.

When Linda called me, the stress Gary felt had become so intense that he was prolonging his Sunday night go-to-bed routine as long as possible in hopes of delaying the end of the weekend (and the start of the school week). This invariably resulted in late bedtimes for Gary, and frequently made him too tired and sick to get to school on time. In every respect, Gary displayed the classic signs of severe bullying: lowered self-esteem, helplessness, depression, and the chronic fearfulness and anxiety that come from living under the near-constant threat of arbitrary attack. His suffering had come to interfere with all aspects of his life, including his mental, social, and emotional development; for example, his enjoyment of school and ability to learn were badly compromised, since he was more concerned with where the next attack would come rather than his studies.

Like many other bullied children, Gary responded to his prolonged terrorization by retreating into a shell. Unfortunately, this sort of self-exile just exacerbates the problem. The only way Gary felt he could control the situation was through avoidance, until he was set on avoiding the greatest threat of all: school. Linda, on the other hand, felt helplessness and guilt because she was unable to shield her child from being hurt or threatened. Like many parents caught in this situation, she found that feeling angry was much safer than feeling powerless and out of control.

The first thing I tried to do was give her the space to express and work past her anger and frustration. And as a parent, you may need to do that with someone—who doesn't have to be a professional psychologist. Any good friend who will listen works just fine. Get out your anger and fears with another adult instead of letting them spill all over your child.

After guiding her toward a more even and reflective tone, I gave Linda some simple tools and problem-solving strategies to help her reach Gary. This began with an emotional "time-out," a half-hour break to allow the intense emotions (on both sides) to dissipate enough for them to have a dialogue. Often, in these situations, what a child needs more than anything else is a powerful, calming presence.

She was then able to re-approach Gary using active listening techniques, this time adopting a more calming tone in order to let him know that she was ready to hear what he had to say, and more importantly, that she wasn't angry with him.

"I'm sorry I lost my cool," she said. "I love you and it sounds like you're having a really rough time right now. Can you tell me more about what's happening with these kids? You don't deserve to be treated that way and we can work on a solution together."

Kids like Gary are often waiting for just such an opportunity, and soon all the feelings he had bottled up for the past several months came pouring out, a torrent of anger, frustration, and fear.

As he confessed the anguish of the recent past, Linda realized that the entire experience had been even worse for Gary than it might have been; while not talking about his fears and feelings was an attempt to smother them, Gary's silence instead allowed them to grow and multiply until they overwhelmed him. She helped Gary see that the same kids—and not an uncontrollable number of kids—were responsible each time. It wasn't that "everyone hated him," as he had grown to believe. This helped contain his emotions and enabled him to believe that as long as they could come up with a solution to stop this small group of kids, he wouldn't feel hated anymore.

His mom went through the questions in the bullyproofing prescription with Gary. "Do I feel powerful enough to confront the bully myself?" No, he didn't. He was at his wit's end and had no confidence in his social ability at this point. He was pretty sure the kids would just make fun of him more if he tried to tell them to knock it off. "Is there any way for me to laugh this off?" Not at that time. It had been too much for too long, and Gary's sense of humor was pretty broken down. "Can I rely on help from others?"

Well, there was a possibility. He hadn't thought about this solution, and it gave him a little hope—maybe there were other kids who would be willing to stand up with and for him if they knew how much it was bothering him. Maybe there were adults who would watch out for him if they knew he wanted them to. It hadn't occurred to him that maybe the reason no adults had intervened was that they didn't know what was happening to him—and that it was okay to tell them, instead of trying to deal with it alone. He was seeing now that his mother could listen, so maybe other adults could help, too. It didn't mean that he was a loser, as he'd thought.

The first order of business was to address Gary's insecurity at school, so we set up a meeting with his teacher and principal to accomplish this. Gary was unwilling to return to what was, for him, a hazardous environment. This behavior, which even some parents interpret as cowardice or meekness, is actually a healthy coping response. Linda worked with Gary's teacher and principal to create "safety zones" and identify "safety people" in the school environment, a stopgap measure to help him feel safe while we began to institute the next phase.

The "safety zones" were places and key people set up by the principal and teacher (teacher's room, principal's office, or being near a particular aide he felt safe with) that he could walk over to during recess and lunch to feel protected. He also knew that the principal would check in with him each day to make sure things were okay. If things weren't, the principal would inform the teacher, and would tell the aggressors that there had been a number of reports from others about their bullying behavior. This way Gary wouldn't feel like he was being further stigmatized as a tattle-tale. With greater documentation of these incidents, the principal also had enough information to contact parents of the bullying kids and ask for their involvement.

Gary's next solution was to ask kids he felt comfortable with to be "real friends" and walk with him to help him feel safe. He taught them how to help him: If they couldn't help him fight off the teasing, he trusted that they would go find a teacher or other adult. This social connectedness is the most important bullyproofing element for any child.

As Gary moved past the crisis stage, he worked on looking and feeling less emotionally vulnerable to others. This afforded him some power to prevent himself from feeling targeted. More importantly, by learning that he could overcome his adversity, he began to develop true self-esteem and resilience, thus making him a less likely target for bullies.

The Steps to Take

Once you know there's a problem, you have to figure out how serious it is and whether or not your child has the ability to handle it without outside help.

The hierarchy of solutions looks something like this:

1. Work with the child to solve it by him or herself.

2. Work with the child to enlist friends to help.

3. Ask a teacher or aide for help.

4. Call the principal.

5. Ask for intervention from a school psychologist or guidance counselor.

6. Talk to other parents of victimized children and approach the principal again if you haven't received the help you need for emotional and physical safety.

7. Approach the superintendent.

8. Use law enforcement if you feel your child is in danger and the school has not been able to protect your child's emotional and physical safety.

9. Use the legal system if all else fails.

Can the Child Solve It?

Of course, the simplest course of action is just to work with the child on proper responses and reactions. Here, you'll use role-playing to figure out how the child normally reacts and where she's going wrong. Ask the child how the bully normally acts—then you play the role of the bully (not *too* aggressively, of course!).

Remember the "power contest." The first order of business is to work on getting the child not to show a strong reaction in any manner. No crying, yelling, arm-crossing, looking down, and so on. You may want to first take the role of a target and show your child what it looks like to give the big reaction. Then show what it would look like not to give a big reaction. Ask them which one made the target look more powerful.

This alone made a very big difference for Anita, a seventeen-year-old girl I worked with. She was just a very shy girl, a little overweight, not comfortable in social situations, and she had been brutalized for years. She excelled academically, but was the brunt of the popular girls' jokes, so she felt worthless in every area of her life except her studies. Even a few girls who had been her friends in earlier years now teased her, because she was at the bottom of the social ladder and no one wanted to take her place.

When she came to me, her parents and I agreed that if things ever got to be too much, there was always the possibility that she could change schools. This way, she wouldn't feel trapped in a hopeless situation. I tried to dissuade them from this as the primary option because she would probably encounter similar problems without the right skill set.

Quickly, I learned that when a group of girls teased her, Anita would often cry, as she did in my office whenever she spoke about the situation. They could bring her to tears just with their dirty looks and under-their-breath comments as she walked by. Sometimes her whole body would shake; that's how fearful and humiliated she was. So the first thing we had to work on was to lose that reaction.

We did it through role-playing. Over and over, we ran through situations where the popular girls would say something awful or laugh at her, and instead of crying, Anita would learn to just hold her ground. She didn't have to say anything or fight back. She could walk away—but she had to walk away with pride. This meant that she had to learn to make eye contact with these girls even as they teased her, and to keep her head up, and to show that they weren't bothering her—even if they were. We talked about that power game of bowling, which she liked, and she focused on those pins standing firm.

This wasn't immediately effective for Anita because her emotions were so entrenched, and she had even reached the point where she wanted to apply to another school whenever she was upset. However, a few weeks later, she decided to stay where she was when she saw that the ongoing onslaught of abuse was diminishing and the girls had begun to loosen up with their attacks. In time, the girls gave up. It took them a while to believe that Anita really wasn't going to fall apart again, and once they believed it, she wasn't a fun play toy for them anymore. All it took was solid nonverbal communication.

Comeback Lines

Comeback lines can be risky if the child isn't good at delivering them. It's best to keep the message pretty simple and not too over-the-top. If you have to use a thesaurus to help your kid think of a comeback, that's not a great sign.

But they can also work wonders. That's what happened with Kevin, a twelve-year-old boy I worked with. He was an artistically inclined kid who was into a lot of activities not typical for boys: dancing and singing, especially. It's almost a given that boys who are into musical theater pursuits will be teased for being "gay" in middle school and high school. Some kids laugh it off and do fine, and others have trouble with it. Kevin was not having any luck brushing it off because he got so angry. Three strikes in a row for the bullies.

In fact, he had already changed schools three years in a row before we met. His parents had talked to the principals, but nothing much changed. Boys who were more into sports and other "manly pursuits" were still tormenting the boy. But Kevin loved what he did—he didn't want to give up performing just because other kids thought it was uncool. So we needed to work out a way for him to do what he loved and not get pummeled for it.

Kevin was an actor . . . so he had to connect with the idea of acting. In the hallways, when boys teased him, he had to "act" cool and unaffected. He had to turn things around. And what worked for him was a short series of comebacks.

When the boys said, "You like to dance . . . you're so gay," Kevin would say, "You think I'm gay? You're the one bringing up that word. Are *you* worried about being gay?"

To another boy who was following him around all the time, Kevin said, "I think it's great that you give me so much attention. I've never had this much attention from someone who likes me this much." When the kid got in his face again, he said, "When I'm successful, are you going to be my manager? Because you seem to want to be around me all the time."

These kinds of lines completely threw the boys. They had no idea what else to say, other than to stammer a bit. They backed off completely.

One of the reasons this strategy worked is that he never got upset and protested their declarations. He didn't need to say, "I'm not gay!" Saying that—whether it was true or not—would just show that he really didn't want them to say he was gay. Instead, joking around and deflecting the comment made it clear that he was not disturbed by whether they thought he was gay or not. It wasn't going to be an issue for him.

By laughing and being strong and putting himself out there, Kevin gained better status in the school. His mother also worked with the principal to assure that Kevin would have some free time during study periods when he could meet other kids who were into

GAIL LYNCH'S STORY

When my son was in elementary school, more than a few years ago, he came home from school with the report that a schoolmate had tried to beat him up in the bathroom. I was concerned, of course, and asked what he'd done to save himself. He said, "Oh, it was easy. I just said, 'You'd better leave me alone. My mother's the PTA President.'" I knew that being the PTA President wasn't exactly a position of authority. But my son didn't really know that and neither did the other kid. I think the fact that he believed that it mattered and conveyed that to the other kid was what stopped the bullying. People are less likely to mess with you when you say something with conviction.

the same sorts of hobbies he was. He found a group of kids he could spend time with, and they helped to boost his confidence and help him feel like he was not alone.

A woman named Maria Ayres remembers that when she was fourteen, a girl in school had been picking on her for six months. Maria had no idea why she was targeted, but she first handled it with avoidance and ignoring the girl—which didn't work. One day, Maria decided not to take it silently anymore. She opened her locker, and as always, the girl came over and slammed the locker door shut.

"I sighed and looked at her, but before she could start, I said to her, 'I want to thank you.' Well, everyone started to laugh. She said, 'Thank me? Thank me for what?' I said, 'For teaching me patience.' Well, everyone stopped laughing. She looked at me like I had two heads and said, 'What the hell are you talking about?' I replied, 'You are teaching me to wait until the good person in you wins out and you act like the person you really are.' Then I waited to get smacked. She just turned away and never bothered me again.

TRACEY ROLFE'S STORY

When I was in grade one at primary school, one of the older girls in the class bullied me. My mom used to give me five cents a day to spend in the school canteen, but rather than spend it, I would put it in my sock and take it home, so I could save up and buy books. Anyway, Geraldine found out about the money and threatened to have her older sister beat me up if I didn't give it to her every day, or if I told anyone that she was making me do this. At first I complied, because I was afraid.

This went on for several weeks, and then I got fed up and decided to call her bluff. Unfortunately for me, though, it wasn't all bluff. Sure enough, her sister (who was a year older than us) and another girl hit and punched me one lunchtime.

After that, I was too scared to go to school, but I was also too scared to tell anyone what was going on. I told my mom I was sick. She looked puzzled, but accepted this—the first day. But the second day, she sat me down and

This is a single incident and I don't know why it worked but I have used words ever since."

Stepping In as a Parent

With younger children, it's sometimes effective for the target's parent to speak directly with the bully. Bullies specifically want children to keep the behavior a secret; a target's silence is coveted, because then the bullying can continue unabated and the bully won't have any consequences. But before the second grade, most children have a great enough fear of having their bad behavior discovered by adults that a parent can put an end to it directly.

It's also possible to talk it through with the bully's parents, *if* you know the parents and are comfortable with them. Do not try asked what was wrong. I said I was sick, and she said that she knew I wasn't, and asked what was going on at school that I suddenly didn't want to go anymore. So I told her, and she said she would take care of it. This frightened me even more, and I still didn't want to go to school, but she bundled me off.

As it happened, parent-teacher interviews were about this time. My mom vaguely knew Geraldine's mom, so with me in tow, she went up to Geraldine and said, "I know what you've been doing to Tracey, and I'm going to tell your mom about it." Then she left me with Geraldine and went to speak with Geraldine's mom. I was petrified. I'll bet now that Geraldine was every bit as scared as I was. Later, my mom told me that she went and spoke to Geraldine's mom about general things: the weather, the school—whatever. She never mentioned the bullying at all, but her ruse was effective. Geraldine never bothered me again.

to approach parents you've never met to bring up a bullying issue; it rarely turns out well. Most will be defensive, and some will be aggressive.

Tracey's story is a great example of several facets of bullying behavior and response. First, note that even in the first grade, Tracey didn't want to tell her mother what was going on. Even after the girl had stolen her money every day for several weeks, and even after two girls physically attacked her, Tracey wasn't coming out with it. Instead, she made up an illness to avoid further punishment by the bullies.

Luckily, by the second day of avoidance, Mom was savvy enough to realize that something was going on, and she coaxed it out of her daughter and set out to take action. The one problem in this equation is how frightened Tracey was about her mom's plan. It's very possible that her mom could have included her daughter in the decision-making process, eased her concerns and reassured her better, or left her with a different group of girls rather than leaving her with Geraldine during that tense meeting. In this case, the resolution was very positive, but it wouldn't have likely worked out the same way if Geraldine had been older, more entrenched as a bully, and/or if she had a better-established "group of bullies" ready to take over her dirty work. But in cases where it's a single, young bully like this, a parent may have success confronting the bully directly or even speaking with a parent, if she knows the parent and asks for her help.

If you don't want to bluff like Tracey's mom did, you could instead say, "If this ever happens again, I'm going to tell your parents (or the teacher, or the principal)."

Asking for Help from Teachers and Principals

When children are young, they're more likely to tell parents and teachers when they've experienced bullying. As they get older, they often think—and rightfully so—that "tattling" will only make things worse. The bullies may exploit this as just another sign of vulnerability, that the kid was so "weak" that he had to run to Mommy and teacher to solve his problems for him. Even if authorities manage to keep the bully away from your child on school grounds, his friends may take up where he left off, and there's no telling what will happen the moment the bully is off school property. Schools are now trying to teach kids the difference between tattling and reporting: Tattling is to get a kid in trouble, and reporting is to get a kid out of danger and into safety. The key is to find a way to help your child not feel alone in her struggle, and to try and help her find a solution.

Try not to assume that you know better than your child, and try not to rush in to save the day. Of course your job is to help problem-solve and to offer solutions that your child may not have thought of, but remember that the bully has already made your child feel less powerful; if you insist on an action your child opposes, you've just made your child feel even more powerless.

Rather than telling your child it's for "his own good," listen carefully and involve him in creating a plan. Assuming your child doesn't feel capable of confronting the bully himself, or has tried and hasn't succeeded, involving a teacher or school administrator may be an important step—but it must be done on terms your child can agree to.

The normal hierarchy is to call the teacher first. If the child has more than one teacher, you may want to approach the one he feels most comfortable with. If the child feels that the teacher is part of the problem, then go straight to the principal.

Unfortunately, not all teachers are bully-savvy. Some are old-school types who believe that bullying is a normal rite of passage, others are trying to be cool and align themselves with the popular students, others think it's somehow a good idea to "toughen up" kids by mocking them in front of the class. And okay, some are just sadistic.

In those cases, you don't want to bother complaining to the teacher, because the child will just feel even more blocked off. The principal is more likely to listen if you can write down very specific dialogue and actions, and not just a general, "And the teacher made fun of him, too!"

But in most cases, the teacher is the starting point—and with any luck, the ending point. If the problems continue, though, you'll need to call in the principal as well.

Confidentiality is key. While some teachers may believe that if they can just get the two kids in a room together, they'll miraculously shake hands and leave as friends, this is beyond idealistic.

Bullies are experts at manipulation, and can usually convince adults that they never meant to hurt anyone. Your child will feel pressured to minimize the bully's bad behaviors and keep the bully out of trouble to save face. Putting kids of uneven power into a room together and telling them to work it out is not appropriate. It terrifies the target and often reinforces the uneven power dynamic. It gives the bully even more information about the target and gives the bully more power, especially if the bully is a chronic offender. Therapists don't talk to domestic violence victims in the same room with their abusers because the power is uneven, and that rule applies with bullying incidents because there is uneven power.

So unless it's what your child wants, you don't want to set up a meeting where the bully will be present, and you don't want the teacher to run back and tell the bully and the bully's parents everything you've said. Privacy is really important to encourage continued reporting and safety for your child, so you must make sure that the teacher understands that everything you say is to be confidential.

You also don't want to walk in angry with the intent of "bullying" the teacher or principal into doing what you want. Remember that your child will learn from your behavior. The way you handle this situation can look just like the bully's behavior if you try to intimidate the teacher, make the principal feel inept, and make heated demands and threats. All you're teaching the child is that you favor bullying behavior, and that using aggression is a desired way to gain power. You can write out a script for yourself about what you want to say, to keep your emotions calmer and in check. The specific behavior you want to address will be in front of you.

You can decide with the teacher or principal if your child needs to be present at this initial meeting. If a situation has occurred where your child isn't safe, it may be a good thing if your child is present. If not and you feel it would overwhelm your child, write down everything he can remember about specific incidents—dates, places, words, actions, witnesses. If your child has come home with bruises or torn clothes, take pictures. If you have seen threatening e-mails or text messages, print them.

Be prepared to face denial of the bullying behavior, proclaimed ignorance of the situation even if you're sure your child has spoken up before, blame-shifting where your child is accused of being too sensitive, and unconvincing claims that they'll "handle it." Be prepared to counter the arguments with specific evidence or probing questions. Be assertive, not aggressive, when you ask the school officials to help enact a plan to stop the problematic behavior. Ask to see a copy of the school's antibullying policy, and to make a photocopy that you can bring home. If there is none, ask why not!

Teachers Who Bully

Just as a teacher who's on top of bullying issues can solve the problem, a teacher who *is* a bully can make it tons worse. The teacher sets the tone about what's acceptable in school; if students see that the teacher uses his power inappropriately, makes fun of students in hurtful ways, or singles out students for ridicule, then they're much more likely to feel entitled to do so themselves. After all, the teacher does it, so it must be warranted.

This leads students to hold the "weaker" kids in even greater contempt. It teaches them that they're better than the targets and that empathy is a sign of weakness. And if it's hard for students to step in and stand up against a peer bully, imagine how tough it is to stand up for someone when it's a teacher doing the bullying.

JANE'S STORY

A few boys in seventh grade bullied me in 1985 in a private Christian school. They would constantly write ugly notes about me and ugly things on the blackboard. They would go in my locker. We had one main teacher who was no help. I was nervous and hearing-impaired so I was an easy target. I was so embarrassed I didn't want to tell my parents, but my best friend told them. My father went to the school to talk to the principal. The principal gathered the boys together for a talk, and they did not bother me again. I don't know what the principal said. From my own experience and from what others say, it seems boys lose their mind when they hit middle school age! I had known most of these boys since kindergarten, and they did not bother me until seventh grade.

If you suspect that a teacher may be a bully, try asking your child questions like this:

- Does the teacher ever say nasty things about anyone in the class?

- Does the teacher ever make a student feel isolated or left out?

- Does the teacher ever give more work to one person than others?

- Does that ever happen to you?

If you find out that a teacher is bullying, take it to the principal, and make sure your child can have a confidential conversation with the principal, away from the teacher.

Sample Antibullying Policy

This is a sample of a school's antibullying policy. Some states require each school to have one, others don't yet—but there's a strong pressure on all schools that haven't adopted one yet. I believe you are entitled, as a parent, to insist on a policy like this one to show that the school understands what bullying is and has taken an active stance against it.

XYZ Elementary School is committed to providing a safe and secure environment for all of its community members and will not tolerate any action or behavior that restricts any person's rights to physical and emotional safety.

DEFINITION OF BULLYING
A repeated and/or chronic pattern of hurtful behavior involving intent to maintain an imbalance of power. What this means is that a bully finds satisfaction in harming people he considers weaker to build up his own sense of power. Bullying can be divided into different types:

Physical bullying: Pushing, shoving, kicking, destruction of property, knocking books out of one's hands, throwing objects at someone, stealing someone's belongings.

Verbal bullying: Words or comments with the intent to hurt someone, including name-calling, mocking, teasing, taunting, racial or discriminatory words, and unwanted nicknames.

Relational bullying: Exclusion from a social group, gossiping, shunning, rumors, or behavior that has the intent to make another feel bad in front of others.

Cyberbullying: The use of hurtful and defamatory information and communication over the Internet (e-mail, IMs), mobile phones, picture phones, blogs, or any other technology with the intent to harm another person.

Responsibility of our community: All members of our community have a responsibility to work toward the prevention and management of bullying. If all members work together to reduce bullying, the safety and comfort of all members will be facilitated.

STAFF
The staff is required to:

- Be positive role models in their behavior at all times.

- Be aware of the types of bullying behavior and consistently vigilant in identifying it.

- Be alert when children are in less supervised areas and more proactive in providing responsible supervision.

- Provide help to targets first.

- Document any bullying activity.

- Report all bullying documentation to the appropriate person handling discipline and consequences.

- Maintain confidentiality of all bullying incidents and reporting by others.

STUDENTS
Students are required to:

- Make a decision to avoid bullying any other person.

- Take a step to alert an adult or help the injured student if bullying occurs.

- Report to an adult in a truthful way to ensure the safety of all students.

- Be a part of a bystander community and do "the right thing" in helping those less fortunate.

PARENTS
Parents are required to:

- Encourage their children to ensure the safety of all students.

- Encourage their children to support any child who feels threatened either during or after a bullying incident.

- Encourage children to report to an adult if bullying occurs.

- Document any report of bullying and contact the school.

- Speak to staff in a respectful manner when contacting the school.

- Encourage children to be caring community members and not be aggressive or retaliatory to others even if they are victimized.

- Accept the school's response to the bullying even if it is not apparent to you immediately.

If bullying occurs:

- The school staff will deal with the incident immediately.

- Staff will document it.

- The staff person in charge of discipline will review and deal with the situation as he or she sees fit.

- Staff will look for patterns of bullying behavior.

- Consequences and discipline will be discussed with the offending child.

- The offending child will be asked to reflect on his own behavior without judgment or blame toward others.

- Support for the target will be given.

- Pupils may experience consequences that include: loss of recess or activity, call home to parent, detention, behavioral contract, community service, restitution, suspension or expulsion (based on severity and chronicity of problem), or other consequences that match the situation.

The goal of this policy is to increase awareness about bullying problems and to bring consistency within the community when managing bullying incidents. The purpose of these measures is to ensure that a strong reporting and documentation procedure is in place, that bullying is dealt with fairly and quickly, and that respect is given to all members of our community. It is essential that confidentiality is maintained and support is provided to both targets and bullies that ensures that all community members involved with such persons are informed of the issues, and that the consequences and discipline provided are commensurate with the bullying incident(s).

How Teachers and Principals Can Help

The last thing you want is for your child to be singled out even more than usual, or for the bully to feel that your child snitched. So instead, work with the teacher or prominent adults in the school to try these options:

- **Help the adults see.** Be specific in letting the teacher know where and when the bullying occurs. Have a staff member just "happen" to walk behind the bully in the lunch room, or ask the teacher to observe through a window at recess. No one can be accused of tattling if the teacher has seen the behavior herself.

- **Identify the "hot spots."** All schools need to focus on the places in school where bullying is most likely to occur. These include the least supervised areas: the lunchroom, recess, hallways, locker rooms, bathrooms, and bus. Make sure that the school's resources are targeting the hot spots and kids who may be victimized.

- **Clearly define the penalties.** In one school district where bullying on buses was a significant problem, the school enacted a program where offenders would have a corner of their bus passes clipped off each time they bullied. When the fourth corner was clipped, they were no longer allowed on the bus and had to find their own rides to school. Complaints went way down and not a single student had a bus pass revoked. Work with school officials to come up with creative plans where the rules are clear and the consequences are spelled out. Older bullies sometimes think it's "cool" to get suspended, particularly when their parents don't care. At what point does the bully get removed from the classroom for good?

- **Make penalties clear to the bully's parents.** Rather than trying to confront the bully's parents on your own, try to have school officials intervene. The only time I encourage parents to call other parents directly is if they already have a relationship. Then you can try to bring them into a problem-solving dialogue: "I need your help. My child told me that our kids had a problem today. Can you try to find out what happened? My child came home really distressed. Do you think you can get back to me so we can try to work it out together?" Sometimes this works, but you need to know the parent involved. Otherwise, the adage "The acorn doesn't fall far from the tree" is unfortunately fitting in many bullying cases. More often than not, the bully's parents will not react the way you hope they will, and you may even feel threatened if you confront them yourself. They will tell you their kid wouldn't do that, or your kid is provoking it, or there's no proof, or you're overreacting and "boys will be boys." Let the principal explain the severity of the problem and what actions will be taken if the bully doesn't stop. See if they'll suggest or require counseling or anger management courses.

- **Enlist compassionate kids.** The teacher may be able to seat your child near kids who are known to be friendly and helpful, or encourage them to partner up in group exercises, to give your child a chance to form a bond with a potential ally who could make your child feel safer. If your child is young, an older "peer mentor" could help.

- **Create check-in times.** At least once a day during the crisis period and once a week afterward, your child should meet with a school official in a private area to discuss any incidents that have happened. Don't expect your child to take the initiative and go to the teacher every time; the teacher or other school official must take a proactive role.

- **Increase supervision.** Some children are so afraid to use the student bathrooms that they'll risk having accidents instead. Bullying flourishes where there is no supervision, like in bathrooms or locker rooms. During the crisis period, check to see if your child can use a faculty bathroom instead, and try to have the physical education teacher or other staff member in the locker room. See if the school will ask for volunteers in the community to ride buses with elementary or middle school kids, or if high school juniors or seniors will sit in the back of a bus or class (and earn community service credits) to keep an eye on things. That's just what a junior high school chorus teacher on Long Island did when he had a cliquish girls' choir; he asked two high school students to visit during their study hall and lunch periods. Younger girls loved to confide in them, and they were able to model good behavior while serving as deterrents to bullies.

- **Create safety zones.** Ask the school officials to work with you to create "sanctuaries" in the school where the child can go if she feels threatened. These could include faculty rooms, the guidance counselor's office, the nurse's office, a music practice room, or anywhere else the child can safely duck into to get out of harm's way and find someone to talk to who knows the situation.

- **Use hidden cameras.** Department stores have them. Convenience stores and banks have them. Why can't a school invest in a few well-placed security cameras to observe what's really going on in the hallways, cafeteria, or playground? One bus camera captured a twelve-year-old being assaulted by several kids taking turns for ten minutes. WISH-TV's I-Team 8 in Indiana did a series on bullying and placed hidden cameras around local schools for two months. They captured horrifying scenes of kids getting hit and shoved, while bystanders laughed and threw things. It prompted a state senator to draft legislation to make Indiana schools more accountable for bullying on school grounds.[18]

- **Ask students to sign a pledge.** Without mentioning your child's situation, encourage the teacher to do role-playing exercises

SAMPLE QUESTIONS TO ASK
A TEACHER OR PRINCIPAL

Who can I count on to make a plan to make my child safe?

What is that plan, and how will the plan be communicated to my child and me?

What should my child do when the behavior she fears recurs?

Are there adults in the school who can handle this? What is their plan of action and discipline if the pattern of behavior repeats itself? What actions are they willing to take to ensure my child's safety and well-being if this continues or escalates?

Are discipline and consequences clear and consistent to the kids? Do children know what will be expected of kids who act out?

Will the teacher have discussions with kids about bullying issues in general?

with students to demonstrate what bullying is and how they can make it stop. At the end, ask each student to sign a pledge affirming that he will not engage in bullying practices, and will stand up for others who are being bullied, or tell a teacher if someone is in danger.

- **Start an anonymous tip box.** Suggest that the teacher place a locked box with a slot on top in a spot children can get to without everyone else in class seeing. This may encourage kids to report bullying incidents they wouldn't otherwise talk about. This can also create a good excuse for a teacher to say that she received several reports about a bully, thus taking the "blame" away from your child. Sometimes the best place for these boxes is in the nurse's station or office.

Would you link my child with others to create protection from the kids who are problematic?

What kind of training has the school staff completed to ensure they understand the problems that children face around bullying? What is their obligation to ensure safety for my child?

On the proactive/positive side:

What can I do to promote better communication with the school and administration?

What kind of reporting procedure would you like me to follow if I hear of these problems occurring? How will I know you have taken this information and acted upon it?

Some teachers are better at talking to students about these sorts of issues than others. Some are able to have open discussions in class about the less-obvious bullying patterns—like teaching kids to communicate directly instead of letting rumors flourish, and knowing where the line is between joking around and hurtful teasing. If the teacher doesn't feel comfortable talking about these issues, then someone else needs to do it. A counselor might be a fine speaker, or the principal might consider hiring a bullying specialist to speak to all students (and faculty, and parents, separately), or in particularly troubled classes.

If you, as a parent, can make these suggestions idiot-proof, all the better. Look up local child psychologists and see if any of them speak about bullying. Look up authors of books like this one, or in-depth articles about bullying, and see if any of them are within driving distance. Pass the contact information to the principal with your suggestions. Try to use your parent-teacher organization as a group to back your interest in these initiatives. Power comes from a bigger group.

Write down the details of any meetings you have with school officials, or use a tape recorder to capture every word. Take notes as they tell you what actions they will take. What will happen if the bullying continues? What disciplinary measures will they use, and when? If the procedures they've offered aren't followed, you can remind them of exactly what was said, and if necessary, take your complaints higher up.

What Doesn't Work

Sometimes teachers mean well, but don't know how to handle bullying situations. One teacher decided to cancel recess altogether rather than deal with the problems that arose. This is not an appropriate solution, because it punishes all kids for the actions of a few bullies, and because it doesn't give the bullies any chance to be held personally accountable and possibly learn from their bad behaviors.

The "boot camp" model, however, can work temporarily. When a new soldier-in-training does something wrong, the whole squad may have to do pushups, run extra miles, clean bathrooms, etc. The idea is that the other squad members will resent the troublemaker, and that the troublemaker will feel pressured not to screw up again, or face the ire of peers. In this same way, recess (or other activities) *can* be canceled for a day or two to make the point and raise the likelihood that kids will keep bullies in check, but after that, it should only be the bullies themselves who are denied privileges.

Some teachers believe it's best for kids to just work these things out for themselves. If that were true, we wouldn't have the bullying problem in the first place. When there is uneven power between kids, they can't be trusted to work things out between themselves. If you're dealing with two former friends, or two kids who are approximately equal in social stature, arguments and fights may be worked out by sending the kids to the school counselor to talk it out. But this is not usually a good idea for children of unequal power. The moment the bully leaves the adult's supervision, you can expect that she'll say something threatening to the target.

Another popular way to handle fights is to punish both people involved, because it just seems too difficult to get to the bottom of who was actually to blame. The principal or dean of students will usually talk to both parties, who'll each say, "He started it!" and sometimes it goes no further—both kids get detention or in-school suspension (or out-of-school suspension, if it's a particularly bad physical fight).

Unfortunately, even if the principal asks witnesses who was to blame, the target stands little chance: the bully is usually more popular, and thus, people will be afraid to point the finger publicly. His friends will back him up, and witnesses may be pressured to lie about how the fight happened. The principal should have an anonymous tip box easily available for situations like this, and should purposely seek out unbiased witnesses—trusted students who aren't buddies of either student—who can help determine if this was a bullying situation versus a fight among "equals."

That is why I always insist on documentation in a school whenever bullying occurs. It is so important for teacher aides, teachers, or office personnel to write down whatever incident they see or hear about to look for patterns of behavior, because bullies can be quite elusive. This documentation reduces the "he said, she said" issue. The more documentation a school encourages, the better bully prevention plan a school has.

For some bullies, there's little punishment that'll be effective.

Some of them actually like the idea of in-school suspension because it means they get to skip class and sit around and doodle all day. Some think it makes them look tougher to be in trouble all the time. Some are worried about a principal calling their parents; others know their parents won't care or won't believe the principal.

Taking away privileges (forcing the child to eat lunch in the principal's office rather than the cafeteria, suspending the child from after-school sports, making the child stay indoors during recess) can work. Humiliation tactics (making the child wear a hat that says, "I'm a bully," making the child sit on display in the front of the room) may work, but usually draw huge protest from parents and from me. I am not an advocate of humiliation as a role-modeling technique.

One that walks the line is making the bully write and read an apology to the class. If this is attempted, the teacher should always approve the written apology before the bully reads it, because it's likely to contain subtle (or not-so-subtle) digs at the target, such as, "I'm sorry I called Francine an idiot, even though she was acting like one." Making the bully apologize publicly can put the target in the spotlight, which is unacceptable; an apology should be general and contain no innuendo, such as, "I apologize for name-calling and acting inappropriately to my classmates and I will not do it again."

Don't Let the Bully Fool Them

School personnel should be trained to recognize that bullies are very socially adept and manipulative most of the time, and will try to shift blame or minimize serious problems.

Excuses like "I was just kidding," "I was just teasing," "It was just meant to be fun," "It was only a joke," and "He took it way too seriously" cannot be accepted. The bully needs to be told in no uncertain terms, "I don't believe that, it's not acceptable, and there are consequences for bullying in this school."

Teachers must be careful not to blame the target for being victimized. In some cases, teachers have even punished students for "tattling" or being a "crybaby," which only reinforces the bully's belief that he's right and justified in tormenting the target, because—hey—even the teacher agrees that the kid is a wimp worthy of scorn! It's open season.

If more than one bully is involved, the teacher or principal should not question them as a group. Question one at a time, without giving them any time to compare notes with each other about what they're going to say, or what the other one already said.

So there's no question about what's acceptable and what isn't, school personnel should consider putting up posters in each classroom and/or in the hallways outlining clearly what is considered bullying and what students should do if they spot it. Teachers can also post a list of unacceptable behaviors next to a list of acceptable behaviors so kids understand what is expected of them.

So What Really Works?

Bullies need to get in touch with their empathy. One way to do that is to give them some time to think about their behavior and not make excuses for it. They need to reflect on what they did without blaming or redirecting toward another kid. Unless bullies can start to think about how their own behavior has affected and hurt another, there isn't much that will change them because they haven't had to face their own emotions. Here are some questions you can ask to have a bully gain awareness:

1. What did you do that got you in trouble?

2. Tell me in your own words what your problem behavior was without telling anything about what the other kid did.

3. Did your behavior cross the line and hurt someone else?

4. If you were that kid, what would you have felt?

5. What were you trying to get out of what you did? Attention, power, a laugh?

6. Is there another way to get what you wanted without hurting someone?

7. What is that way?

8. How can you really make the other kid know that you made a mistake?

Remember, girls who bully have a difficult time dealing with their feelings, so they need someone who can be supportive and direct with them so they can learn how to verbalize how they feel without being indirect and hurting the relationships they have with other girls.

Peer Leaders

Many schools have some kind of peer leadership group. They might be called peer mediators, peer mentors, or similar terms. Their function is not always the same from school to school, but many schools expect their peer leaders to be role models and to intervene on behalf of students who are being bullied.

Some schools even start clubs specifically for this purpose. A letter from two teachers to the New Jersey newspaper *Courier-Post* reads, "I'd like to take the time to commend the students of Pine

Hill Middle School. Many of our students decided they were tired of bullies intimidating and harassing other students. They have taken a proactive stance against bullying, and their actions have evolved into a group called Violence Is Preventable.

"The group is made up of two teacher facilitators and more than 100 students. These students all own T-shirts, designed by themselves, which have the VIP logo on the front. All students in the school are encouraged to approach these leaders should they need support."

The teachers go on to say that the "VIPs" designed motivational posters around the school, helped to organize assemblies in the school to promote peace, video-conferenced with elementary schoolkids to teach them antibullying skills, and more. "We all agree that no student should ever be in fear of coming to school. We offer support for victims of bullies and encourage students who are bullies to rethink their behavior and develop respect and empathy which are invaluable character traits."

The truth is that peers are going to see more than teachers will. When kids see adults around, their behavior changes. They straighten up and act a lot different than they do when they believe no one in authority is watching. Peer leadership groups can bridge this gap.

I don't think it's fair for parents to expect their kids to be good bystanders all the time and put themselves into high-risk situations. Asking bystanders to confront bullies alone is high-risk. There are some kids who'll do it, just because that's who they are. They have extremely high empathy and are more upset about injustice than about the risk to their own emotional or physical safety. But this is not something we can expect or ask of our kids. Teaching them to be "good bystanders" doesn't always mean sticking their neck out in the middle of a crisis. How many adults can do that?

But a group of kids confronting a bully is a much lower-risk

SCHOOL COP SOFTWARE

Encourage the principal to download the free "School Cop" program at www.schoolcopsoftware.com to help map where bullying incidents are happening and observe patterns, to figure out where more supervision is necessary.

situation. There *is* safety in numbers. When a group confronts a bully, he doesn't have a clear target for retaliation. A group of bystanders can also take different roles: a few can support a target, while another gets an adult or peer leader to help.

Peer leadership groups need to be trained. School counselors, teachers, or principals may serve as the advisors for the group, and teach them what is expected of them. They may be entrusted with reporting bullying incidents to faculty members, walking kids who are targeted to and from classes to make sure they're safe, inviting kids who are isolated to sit with them at lunch, acting as "buddies" for targeted kids to confide in when they need help, and so on.

At some schools, peer leaders get special privileges along with their special responsibilities. At one New York school, the "top-rated" peer leaders all got permanent hall passes to use whenever they needed them. Peer leaders might also get special access to an unused classroom or office where they can talk to fellow students when they need to. These programs work best when peer leaders have their own strong code for discipline that is maintained strictly, so if they cross the line themselves, they lose their privileges for a period of time.

Clique-Busting

A simple, effective way to challenge the social segregation prevalent in schools is to help kids get to know kids they wouldn't normally speak to. Encouraging these "community building" days sets the stage for acceptance of others in your school.

One program designed to do this is the "Mix-It-Up at Lunch Day," a day where students are assigned seating in the cafeteria, rather than picking their usual seats. Seats may be assigned in a number of ways—by handing students candy bars with their table number on it as they walk in, organizing tables according to students' birth months, giving out construction paper "tickets" to match the color of the tablecloth at their table, and so on.

Many schools make a real event of this day, giving out T-shirts so students can collect signatures from the kids they sit with, putting up posters about the event, having staff members entertain with musical instruments, decorating the cafeteria with streamers and balloons, and having a special dessert.

Teachers and parents can find more information and activity packs at www.mixitup.org.

Similar ideas can be applied during other parts of the day, too. Instead of just sitting around for ten minutes during homeroom or reading silently during study hall, students can be asked to pair off and "interview" each other with sets of questions the homeroom teacher comes up with to break the ice. Students can be set up in groups and asked to talk with each other about given subjects, then "pop quizzed" on these subjects afterward ("Johnny's favorite movie is _____. Sarah's favorite place is _____."). Those who score well on these pop quizzes may get some kind of prize: stickers and badges work well for younger kids; a free snack or grab-bag-type item may be better for older kids.

The objective here isn't to get bullies and targets to become best friends, but it's a way for targets to find social connections to shield them from the bullies. An isolated child is an easy target, and it's unlikely for children to stand up for someone they don't know. And a child who's being shunned by her normal group may not have any idea where else to turn. These kinds of opportunities can help to introduce kids who'd get along great if only they weren't normally part of different social circles—and to give shy kids an organized way to speak up and meet people.

It's more important than ever to have supervision during events like this, however—because it is possible that a bully and a target will be seated at the same table in the cafeteria (where normally, they'd be across the room from each other), or paired up together in one of these exercises by accident. An adult needs to be unobtrusively eavesdropping.

Away from the Group

A girl who's become a target of a popular bully may feel like she's being bullied by a whole group of girls. In truth, it's probably one or two main bullies, a few henchmen, a few who will laugh but won't join in, and a few who don't like the behavior but won't speak up out of fear. It's rarely the case that the whole group is equally cruel and that none of them has empathy.

On an individual basis, away from the group, all except the main bullies and henchmen may be decent and even friendly to the target. If the girl is confident enough, she might try approaching one of the girls who seems most sympathetic and saying to her, "If they pick on me, I know it might be hard for you to say anything in front of the other girls, but if I could talk to you afterwards, I would feel better."

If she can find this sympathetic link, it's a good idea to keep that line of communication open. She can also ask the girl to find a teacher or aide if the situation ever gets out of control. It's important not to expect too much, though—expecting the girl to stand up to the bully for her is like asking her to become the new target. Encourage a school to have their counselors do "lunch bunches": having groups of girls get together to learn to communicate with each other directly. If girls can learn to speak to each other about jealousy, anger, and competition in a safe environment, they can learn new skills to reduce the indirect nature of bullying.

Changing Classes or Moving to a New School

Sometimes, school officials will suggest moving your child to a different class or different school. This is rarely a good solution, for two main reasons:

1. It puts the responsibility on the target. Why should the target have to move? Why not the bully?

2. Neither the bully nor the target has gained from the experience. The bully gets the satisfaction of driving away his prey (thus feeling even more powerful), and the target remains vulnerable. The other kids are left to believe that the teacher favored the bully, enforcing the belief that bullying gives you power.

It's a cop-out solution for the school district, because they don't have to deal with the "messiness" of either fixing the problem for good or expelling a child or convincing his parents to move him to a different school. And almost certainly, the bully will simply move on to a new target, learning that he's untouchable.

But sometimes the solution sounds good to parents, who often assume that if they just get their children into a new school, all will be fine. The problem is that once your child has been bullied, it's almost as if she has a neon sign over her head alerting the bullies at the next school. Putting aside the fact that children hear rumors and may well find out that she left her last school because of bullies (Aha! An easy target!), she is likely feeling vulnerable, hasn't developed true self-esteem, and won't know any new friends or confidantes at the new school. Being the "new kid" makes her an easier target by itself.

If at all possible, the goal is to keep your child where she is and create an environment where the bullying cannot thrive any longer. Find out from the teacher where the "nice kids" hang out and encourage your child to talk to them. See if there are any particular clubs or after-school activities where your child may fit in and meet the kinds of friends who'd be willing to speak up for your child and create a bully buffer. Work out deadlines with the school, and be prepared to take further action if the problems continue. Again, you're modeling behavior for your child. Show your child that bullying is unacceptable, that you will not stand by and let it continue, and that you will assert yourself until the problem is resolved.

Remind the school officials that they are required by law to keep your child safe. If this means they need to hire extra personnel just to follow around the aggressive kids, then that's what they need to do. If it means rescheduling the other students' classes entirely, that's what they need to do. If it means having an aide walk the bullies out of the building and directly onto their bus to make sure they can't get into fights as soon as they walk out the door, that's what needs to be done.

School officials would rather inconvenience the conciliatory person; they know darn well that bullies' parents are going to be harder to deal with. They know that when they call to say that their child is no longer allowed to ride the bus, or that their child must have an entirely new schedule to keep him away from the children he's harassing, that kid's parents are probably going to put up a stink and say "Not my kid" or "Not his problem" or "If the other kid has a problem with it, move her!"

They also have to balance their responsibility to educate the bully with their responsibility to protect your child. It's very unlikely for a school to expel a child who is not physically violent, and still unlikely for them to expel a child who *is* violent, unless the violence involves weapons, is demonstrably repeated numerous times on school grounds, or happens under similarly dire situations. Most often, they will try to keep the other child in place.

If this happens and you feel that your child is being "punished" for being a target, you need to remind school officials that your child is not the aggressor, and there is no reason to remove her from her regular activities. Perhaps put the same story in the context of two adults and ask the principal how he'd deal with it

PARENT CHECKLIST FOR SCHOOLS

1. Have I documented all the incidents that I know about in writing? Dates, times, who was involved? What children saw the incident, what adults may have seen it?

2. Do any school personnel know about the incident? How was it handled? Obtain information from the child and adults involved.

3. Have I read my school's code of conduct and become familiar with it?

continues . . .

4. Have I calmed myself enough to have a discussion that is clear and constructive without becoming too aggressive myself?

5. Is this a first-time incident and is it severe enough for school contact versus working with my child first?

   A. If a first incident, who should I contact first?
      i. Teacher: Through phone call and note, and ask for this to be confidential.
      ii. Has teacher responded to me within twenty-four hours? If not, go to principal.
      iii. Principal contact in addition to teacher? Only if it is so serious that significant emotional or physical safety is at issue.
      iv. Other school personnel? Only if incident involved someone in the school who may have been present (monitor, lunch lady, etc.). Ask the school if I have permission to contact one of these staff members.

   B. If this is the second or third contact, and this has happened before with the same kids:
      i. Contact teacher again with phone call and note.
      ii. Ask for phone meeting with teacher.
      iii. Ask for phone meeting with the principal, or send note in to principal with an explanation of the situation.
      iv. Ask what strategies teacher has used to handle this. How effective or ineffective was the intervention?
      v. Can there be a private meeting with my child (if the child feels okay about this and it is confidential) to come up with a plan?
      vi. Ask for feedback from teacher/principal weekly, or even daily if my child is fearful of a situation recurring.
      vii. Are there any other ideas they can provide for my child that will not stigmatize my child further?

6. Have I written down details about each conversation with school staff and stored them in a notebook or well-marked file?

then—if he had two teachers, and one was just trying to do her job while the other followed her around to torment her, stole her money, knocked her down (fill in your scenario here), which teacher would he keep and which one would he fire?

When the System Fails: A Tragic Example

Here's an extreme example of what can happen when children in school are not protected. This is a very serious story and very rare, thank goodness, but nonetheless, it is true.

According to his former principal's testimony, Jonathan Miller got into trouble thirty-four times in his two years in middle school before killing thirteen-year-old Josh Belluardo by "sucker-punching" him in the back of the head as the two got off a bus in suburban Georgia. Belluardo died of a severed artery after lying comatose in a hospital for two days.

Miller had been suspended and placed in in-school suspension multiple times for assaulting students and swearing at a teacher. But after thirty-four incidents that teachers knew about (and potentially many more that they didn't), the problem was allowed to escalate until his target died.[19]

This is a tragic example of what happens when authority figures refuse to acknowledge that their usual methods aren't working. Luckily, most school bullies are nowhere near this extreme, but if you're dealing with a persistent one, you must become persistent yourself.

When you address the school principal for the second or third time on the same issue, be sure to go over what measures have already been tried and make it clear that those measures have not worked and you expect the school to now move on to the next step. Explain that your child is in danger and that the school is legally required to provide a safe environment—which means coming up with a new solution to keep that bully far away from your child.

Last year, I worked with a sixth grader who was tormented constantly by a bully. The school tried a number of interventions, but what finally worked was total separation. The guidance department rearranged the schedules so the boys wouldn't have classes anywhere near each other, and wouldn't even have to pass each other in the halls. A number of adults were told to watch for these kids. They basically had no interaction for the rest of the year, and that solved the problem.

If you are having serious concerns about your child's safety, don't keep banging your head against a wall if you realize that the teacher and principal aren't taking you seriously. Move on to the superintendent. Chances are, the superintendent will just refer you back to the principal—but it will be much harder for the principal to brush you off now. He or she will have to report to the superintendent about the issue, which means he'll need to come up with *something*. If that doesn't work, go to the school board.

Banding Together

One of the most effective ways to make sure the school takes action is to band together with other parents. A principal may brush it off when one parent reports a bullying problem; it might be an anomaly. But when two, three, or more parents report problems with the same kid or group of kids, it's harder to ignore.

The first step is to ask your child if other kids in school are being bullied, too—particularly by the same person or people who are bullying your child. Ask him to pay attention in school and notice who else is getting picked on. Many school districts pass out a "parents list" in the beginning of the year, giving the names and phone numbers of students and their parents. If not, you can try looking up the parents in the phone book, or on switchboard.com. If you're unable to find a listing, call the school's secretarial staff and explain that you'd like them to please deliver a message to So-and-So's parents that you'd like to speak with them. The secretary should be willing to contact the parents to give them your phone number.

You can also try attending PTA meetings and class events and just bringing up the subject to see what other parents have to say about it. You may find a lot of support, or you may find none. Having the PTA approach the principal to address the issue of bullying often makes more of an impact than one parent complaining.

Similarly, you could ask the principal to call a meeting. Ask the principal to invite parents to come discuss the issue of bullying to find out where and when it's occurring, and which students are perpetrating it most often. A meeting like this could be a real eye-opener for the principal and parents. This is exactly how I'm often called in to speak; parents bring up their concerns, and the principal calls me to discuss the bullying problems and work on solutions.

Whether you have a "guest speaker" on the topic or not, it is quite reasonable to expect a principal to occasionally invite parents to meet and discuss important school issues. Considering that nearly all school shootings have been blamed, at least in part, on retaliation for bullying, school officials should understand that bullying is a serious concern that can't be swept under the rug.

Many schools now have policies to have a certain number of meetings and training sessions on this topic every year, instead of waiting for complaints to crop up. All teachers, aides, coaches, and other school personnel attend two or three training sessions in the beginning of the year to discuss what bullying is and how to handle it, parents are invited to come to meetings a couple of times a year to discuss any problems that arise, and kids get "bully training" both in their individual classrooms and in schoolwide assemblies. This is a proactive way to deal with the problem, recognizing that bullying always exists at any school, rather than waiting for a horrible tragedy before coming up with plans for what to do "next time."

Talking to Police

If your child has been the target of physical or sexual violence, it is appropriate to inform local police and file a report. It's also appropriate if your child is being threatened with physical violence. Be sure to bring any evidence you have, such as e-mails, phone messages, pictures of bruises, ripped clothing, and so on. While you should also still inform the school, in cases where safety is a serious concern, the police need to be aware of the situation.

In April 2006, one high school student in Cincinnati who threatened to bring in a gun to kill a classmate was ordered to report to a probation officer, observe a 6 p.m. curfew, take anger management classes, complete twenty hours of community service, and pay court costs.[20]

Talking to a Lawyer

I bring up this subject with some hesitation, because I hope that parents really will look at this as a last resort, but sometimes it is justified to seek legal remedies to bullying problems.

If your child is suffering violent or sexual attacks at school, the school, the bully, and/or the bully's parents may be held liable. Laws differ from state to state as to who may be held responsible and under what circumstances, so you'll need to seek legal advice in your state.

In 2005, eighteen-year-old Dylan Theno sued his former school district, saying that he'd been subjected to bullying for five years, until he finally dropped out of school in his junior year and sought psychiatric help, and the school never intervened. The jury found that he was the subject of gender-based harassment (he was called "fag" and "queer" and other sexual slang words), that this deprived him of his education, and that the school district showed indifference toward the problem. In fact, in court, the school officials said that the boy brought some of the bullying problems onto himself. The jury awarded Dylan $250,000.[21]

In Connecticut in 2005, the parents of a young girl also filed suit against the school district for not addressing the near-daily torment their child faced. They settled out of court—they were not seeking money, but were seeking an apology and revisions to the school antibullying policies, which they got. The parents were very happy with the outcome, saying that school officials did address the problem and that their daughter was doing well.[22]

Nobody Knows Better Than You

Parents sometimes ask me if it's okay to pull their children out of school if the bullying gets too bad. Your best compass in these situations is going to have to be your child. Of course, the goal is to do whatever it takes to clean up the problems, make your child feel emotionally and physically safe, and have the child learn resilience. But there does come a breaking point, and as a caring parent, you're probably the best judge of where that is.

Even as adults, sometimes we all need "personal days"—days we take off of work or just slack off because we're not in the right frame of mind to deal with the day. If your child is so terrorized that you feel like you're sending her off to an executioner, you may feel it necessary to let the child stay home for a day or two while you talk to school officials and get them to make some changes so she'll feel safe on her return. But make this a real "crisis-only" option; if your child learns that she can bust out a few tears and say that someone was mean to her and you'll let her stay home, it reinforces her target role and teaches her that she never has to learn how to deal with the problem.

Be aware that changing schools is not often helpful unless the stigmatization of your child is so severe that even a positive change in them continues to bring more bullying and little change. You might like to think that these bullies at this particular school are crazy, and that everyone else at every other school would treat your child nicely—but it's probably not so. A child who's a target at one school tends to be a target at the next school, too. There are exceptions: A woman tells about a very racist climate in a particular region, where her children were the only nonwhite students in their classes, and were both tormented. Not only that, but they were both becoming violent in response. She was shocked that her daughter, who she describes as a very quiet and obedient girl, was getting into physical fights. The following year, she moved them both to more ethnically diverse schools in a new area, where they flourished. And sometimes, just ditching an old reputation that no longer fits does help.

If you're considering moving the child to a new school, consider bringing the child for counseling first, to work on self-esteem and make the child a less likely target at the new school, so it can genuinely feel like a fresh start and not a proof of failure. I've seen this work many times, especially when kids who are bullied are given new skills so they see they have a new chance at a new school.

Homeschooling or private tutoring is always an option, but of course that can make kids who already feel rejected by their peers even more socially isolated and even less likely to gain confidence in their ability to stand up for themselves, make friends, and learn resilience. If you choose to homeschool, consider doing it for a limited time (maybe one school year) and making sure the child has other outlets for meeting peers.

Children should never feel terrified by the thought of facing bullies at school. It's important to have frank discussions with your child about how serious the problem is and how much it hurts. It's devastating that many parents were unaware or only marginally aware of the fact that their kids were being bullied when those kids committed or attempted suicide. If you're seeing signs of serious depression—withdrawal from activities, crying, mood swings, listlessness, cutting or burning their skin, frequent vague illnesses or excuses to get out of school, isolation, changes in sleep or eating habits, and so on—get to the bottom of it yourself, or make sure your child has a counselor to talk to.

As important as school is, it's never worth a child's life. Your child has a right to feel safe in school, and as a parent, you have the right to demand that school officials live up to this obligation.

FIVE

Bullying in Sports
KEEPING BULLIES OUT OF BOUNDS

As constructive as sports participation can be for a child, this environment has proven particularly hospitable to bullying. This is because bullying is ultimately all about power, and the adrenaline and competition of sports make it a "power rush" for many people, including professional athletes who are well beyond testing out bullying behaviors. When you see footage of Mike Tyson biting a chunk out of someone's ear, or hockey players knocking each other unconscious, or baseball and basketball players jumping into the stands and throwing punches at fans, you've probably seen some out-of-control adrenaline.

We teach kids to be aggressive on the sports field, but we then expect them to turn it off and show "good sportsmanship" as soon as they walk off the field. That's not easy for adults to do, much less kids, who are less adept at controlling their emotions. It can be very difficult to switch from one gear to the other, and some people—like Mike Tyson—seem incapable of ever turning off the aggression.

Behavior on the sports field can be divided between "fair play" (appropriate behavior and good sportsmanship) and what I call "foul play" (bullying and inappropriate behavior that marginalizes others). On the playing field, a fine line exists between competitive play and bullying. The "Bully Spotter" tool on page 162 defines the types of bullying in sports to clarify where that line lies.

Trash Talk

Trash talk is the term for insults and teasing meant to break a player's concentration and throw him off. You'll see it even in friendly play, where a group of buddies are playing baseball and the catcher wises off to the batter: "Go ahead and miss again. Hurry up and strike out, you klutz."

Trash talk can be fun and motivational and part of good-natured competition, but it all depends on how it's used and how the players react. When someone trash talks and the targeted person trash talks right back, you can be reasonably sure you're seeing teasing between equals—and that's no big deal. Or if the targeted person shrugs it off, it's probably fine. It becomes a problem when it's deteriorating a person's morale, however.

People with empathy use their own judgment to read a person's reaction and realize when they've pushed it too far. Then they back off. Sports shouldn't be about destroying someone. But sometimes that point gets lost when kids start believing that winning is more important than being decent human beings. Winning is seen as a goal in which the ends justify the means, so if it takes someone's destruction to get there, it's thought to be excusable.

BULLY-SPOTTER GUIDE
Bullying in Sports

	Mild	Moderate	Severe
Physical	• Hitting, slapping, heckling with intent to hurt	• Illegal use of arms, legs, hands on playing field	• Physical violence to deliberately inflict pain
	• Head butting	• Throwing ball at player with intent to hurt	• Holding player down against his/her will
	• Towel snapping	• Tripping	• Breaking/ damaging property
	• Throwing objects at someone	• Striking with equipment	• Graffiti that defaces property
	• Taking possessions (clothes, equipment, etc.)	• Spitting on purpose	• Locking in a room
		• Holding someone in shower or taking clothes with intent to harm	• Inappropriate, unwanted sexual touching

	Mild	Moderate	Severe
Relational	• Targeting an individual in the locker room • Critical comments meant to hurt • Blame placing; gossiping • "Talking trash" • Dirty looks meant to hurt • Excluding or isolating another player	• Exclusion more than once • Embarrassing a person in front of others • Setting the person up to look foolish/ take blame • Threatening to reveal personal information • Gossiping with intent to isolate • Mild ethnic slurs • Obscene gestures • Using the Internet* for any of the above	• Shunning a player from a team; isolating someone through rumors (or untrue comments to the media) • Hurtful ethnic slurs • Using the Internet* for any of the above

continues . . .

	Mild	Moderate	Severe
Verbal	• Poking fun • Inappropriate language toward others; comments on sexual preferences • Name-calling without hurtful intent • Use of a nickname when told not to • Verbal rudeness to authority • Unwanted sexual comments • Verbally insulting fans	• Verbal threats of aggression against person, property, or possessions • Putting down others • Name-calling with hurtful intent or rudeness • Taunting • One-time sexual harassment • Using the Internet* for any of the above	• Verbal threats to harm person or possessions • Threats of/or retaliation for reporting bullying • Verbal threats of violence or inflicting bodily harm • Escalating rudeness towards others • Ongoing sexual harassment • Verbal abuse toward coach, referee, fans • Using the Internet* for any of the above

*Internet: Includes e-mail, websites, instant messages, phone text messages.

That point was driven home to me one day as I sat and watched a Little League game. A very good pitcher threw a couple of bad pitches, and the opposing team in the dugout lined up and began jumping on the fence and relentlessly tormenting him. They laughed and screamed and made him feel terrible, and to my dismay, their coach was egging them on.

The pitcher lost control of himself and broke down in tears on the mound. It was an awful sight, made all the worse by the fact that these kids thought they had achieved their goal by "breaking" him, and that the coach approved. This kid was upset for a long time, and I don't think this kind of bullying was a character builder. It was meant to disrupt his confidence, and it achieved its goal. I still wonder what the coach was thinking, and if this had been his own son, would he have had any empathy for his child? The probable answer was that he saw this bullying as a character-building exercise and did use this on his own son. The problem here: Teaching bullying behavior promotes poor sportsmanship.

If a coach doesn't step in, kids will take it as a sign that their trash talking is acceptable. That's why it's important for adults to be on the alert, to notice when a player is in distress. But sometimes, it's the coaches who are leading the bullying.

Let me make a point about teams that allow boys and girls to play together, which seems to be happening more often. The important thing here is the attitude of the coach directing the players. A coach who sees the value of the sexes equally sets the example for the team and discourages bullying and social laddering. A coach who has his own issues about the equality of the sexes playing together sets an example that can seriously divide the team and create a "second class" of athlete who falls below the standard.

I remember a great soccer coach who treated all of his male and female players without gender bias, and this team had fun and played like a group of kids who enjoyed playing. On the other side was a coach who rolled his eyes whenever the girls missed the ball (although he never rolled his eyes when the boys made a bad play), and there was the picture of a fragmented team, with the girls huddled together away from the boys and the boys feeling angry when one of the girls did well and they didn't. This experience only reinforced a negative stereotype of sportsmanship for these athletes, and many did not enjoy their sports experience after this.

Problematic Coaches

Kids take their cues from the coach, above all else. If a coach is a bully, the kids will learn that bullying is accepted. That happens more often than we'd like to imagine.

Coaches can bully their players in various ways. They may use insults ("You stink!" "Are you brain dead?"), or physically bully by shoving or slapping kids, or punish them by making them overexert themselves physically (such as holding a "punishment practice" after an exhausting game, or making the team do excessive numbers of pushups or laps around the field). The coach may even encourage hazing behavior, telling the older players to get the younger players "up to speed" about how things are done.

I watched a coach terribly bully a traveling soccer team that hadn't often played together. They were getting whipped pretty badly in the first half of the game, and instead of trying to build them up, this coach tore them down.

"This is the worst team I've ever seen!" he said. "What a lousy effort. You're embarrassing yourselves out there! None of you deserve to be playing travel soccer!"

This was his way of motivating the team. Some coaches believe that they can make a team rally by making them angry. That they can wake the team up and somehow make them play better by just yelling at them. The thing is, I've never seen it work.

In this case, the team, which was already doing poorly in the first half, totally fell apart in the second. They couldn't have been more demoralized. There was no teamwork at all; they weren't even speaking to each other or calling out to one another. They just barely got through the rest of the game. Their interest in passing to each other got lost, they started fouling the other team even more, and more important, they looked morally shot on the field following this team meeting. Kids remember the last thing they are told by the coach, and in this case, they started to play even lousier.

In contrast, I've watched a coach who is truly masterful at the "half-time talk." After a similarly bad first half with his team, he pulls them aside and finds positive things to talk about.

"What do you think we've done well so far? Who did a great job out there? Who showed good teamwork? Who wants to be the one who can go out there and score the next goal? Who wants to lead this team to win this game? Do you think we can do it? Everyone put your hands in the middle and scream the name of our team as loud as you can on the count of five. You guys have it in you."

What a difference. These kids were motivated because they felt like the coach believed in them and that they could be winners. By not focusing so much on the critical aspects, the coach managed to keep the game fun and to help the kids do their best.

I remember a coach who had it just right. In junior high school, two bullies made it their "fun" to throw basketballs at Steve when the coach wasn't around because they felt he wasn't as good as they were. Somehow, the coach must have known that something was up because Steve behaved differently when those two kids were around. Steve explained that he'd never forget how the coach helped him by teaching him to make one great shot. What he did was have Steve practice one shot over and over again with the idea that Steve would have his chance to be a hero and prove to these two brutes that "team" play was more important than anything else.

During their first game of the season, they were up by one point with twenty seconds left when the coach asked Steve to go in the game. Steve remembers feeling like this was going to be his chance, and he'd put the game on ice if he could make his shot. As the ball was passed to him by a teammate he had practiced with all season, he shot his layup, the ball went in, and the team (including the two bullies) hugged him. Steve had never felt like such a winner before. The coach talked to the guys about "team" work and Steve knew that he wouldn't be targeted again. He was right!

Some coaches have naturally positive styles, while others can be brutal. It's important for coaches to remember that very few kids are going to wind up playing professional sports, so the main goal has to be enjoyment. Could there be a clearer message for parents who watch their kids in sports?

That message was apparently lost on Mark Reed Downs Jr., a former T-ball coach who is about to stand trial for allegedly bribing a seven-year-old to hit an autistic child in the face so he wouldn't be able to play in the playoff game and harm the team's chances of winning. The seven-year-old hit the boy in the face and groin with a baseball, and when the target's mother asked why, he explained that the coach offered him $25 to do it.[23]

While most coaches are nowhere near so cruel, many are caught up in the desire to win games, and may look for excuses not to play the weaker players, or to discourage them in the hopes that they'll quit. They may also vent their frustrations on the kids inappropriately if they're worried about losing their job because of a losing streak, or even just having their pride wounded by not being able to coach a team to victory. There can be a lot of pressure on a coach to win games. His higher-ups may not see what he's done to boost morale and build team leadership; they may just see wins and losses and decide his worth as a coach based on that.

When parents see that a coach is being too harsh with kids, or too negative, the best way to deal with it is as a group. It's helpful if you can join with other parents and approach the coach together with a polite message.

"We think you do a great job of teaching the kids, but when you criticize them, it doesn't have a great impact on the kids. Can you think about a more positive approach to motivate them? Because we have seen them really try with praise."

As parents, be specific with any complaints, so the coach understands exactly what behavior is problematic. Don't tell the coach, for example, that he is awful, if you can break down your complaint in a simple way. For example, if he singles out children for criticism in front of their teammates, that could be handled better by simply talking to the children one-on-one instead. It's harder for children to absorb even constructive criticism when they're being held up in front of the team as a bad example.

A more constructive way for a coach to deal with criticisms would be to do so without naming names. Coaches who don't "target" specific kids can rally a group more effectively.

"I saw a few problems in the last game, so let's go over our techniques. Some of you are hesitating too long before you start running . . ." Then comes a demonstration of what he means and how to fix it.

As a parent, you want to protect the child's interest in sports, which means not allowing anyone to ruin the experience by making it feel like too much pressure, or a place for humiliation or bullying. Often, the coach will be receptive to your suggestions, and you should always go to the coach first if possible. If this is not successful, you can take it to the next level. If this is a school program, the next level would probably be an athletic director, then the principal. If it's outside of school, you'll go to the governing body, such as the director of activities for the town.

If you're going to go beyond the coach, however, it's important to have your complaints documented. Write down names, dates, specific quotations, specific incidents, and who witnessed the events. Get together with other parents, if possible, and write down their complaints, too. The more details you can provide to a governing organization, the better chance you have of getting a satisfactory resolution.

You may even be helping to take pressure off the coach. Sometimes, the coach's boss may have lost sight of what the kids and parents actually want (fun!) and have added to the problem with the coach by putting too much pressure on him to win games. Talking about the excessive pressure on the kids may help them realize that priorities need to shift.

Out-of-Control Parents

One of the more disturbing trends in sports is the tendency for parents to become violent or abusive. I was in the stands when a parent actually ran out onto the field and knocked over an umpire because of a bad call. There are similar stories of parents fighting with coaches, other parents, and the kids if you were wondering if my experience was an isolated event. In fact, when I attend sports conferences, I hear stories about parents behaving badly quite often, and setting the worst example for their children.

Surely, there has always been an element of parents living vicariously through their children; parents who were active in sports want to see their children do at least as well as they did, but preferably better. Much like "stage parents" and "pageant moms," these parents may push their kids to succeed even if the kids are not particularly interested. But that doesn't explain the increase in parental aggression in recent times. I have a couple of main thoughts about why some parents have lost their way when it comes to sports:

First, there is increasing competition to get into college, and sports offer a chance for scholarships and acceptances into better schools. Once they've heard stories about recruiters coming to games and offering the sun and moon to the best athletes, it makes parents take the game much more seriously. They want their kids to win at all costs.

Second, what we see on television has normalized bad behavior in the stands. Professional sports have become more violent and chaotic, and we're used to seeing drunken fans get into fistfights. We're used to seeing fans throw things at players and umpires. We're used to hearing fans shout out expletives and threats. Therefore, it's not as jarring as it should be to see parents mimic this behavior at their kids' ball games. The lines between "spectator" and "player" are blurred; instead of remaining in the stands and cheering, fans think they can cross the boundaries and really be part of the game.

The realm of what parents will deem acceptable in sports is a lot different from what they'll accept in other environments. Many will accept having adults yell at their kids, and accept that their kids yell out horribly insulting things to the opposing team, and even jab or kick other kids. Taken out of this environment, those same behaviors would be unacceptable.

People don't often flinch when a high school football coach calls out, "Don't be such a girl!" or "What the hell are you doing?" Now imagine a science teacher saying the same thing in the classroom. There's really no reason why one should be any different from the other, however. These are still adults in authority dealing with kids, and they should be held to the same standards.

Similarly, you don't see parents walking around a classroom during parent-teacher night criticizing other kids' art projects—but you do hear parents complaining and mocking when a kid on a basketball team misses a shot.

Ryan (a client of mine) played Little League baseball when he was in grade school, and he was one of the weaker hitters on the team. His father would talk about his perspective of the game from the stands, and how he'd dread the reactions when his son was up to bat. If he would miss at the plate, you could hear the other parents sighing and grunting, see them rolling their eyes and exchanging irritated glances. It was like being at a class reunion where the popular kids from school still think they're pretty hot, and they sit together and whisper and laugh at the unpopular people. Sports parents can be just like that, with a similar pecking order. The parents of the good athletes may patronize the parents of the lesser athletes, and often let it be known that they don't want the less athletic kids on the team to hold back their little stars.

Of course, this further divides the two groups. The better athletes get treated like kings and queens, and their confidence flourishes. The lesser athletes play less, get made fun of, and their confidence dissolves until they don't want to practice and don't want to play because they associate sports with pressure and embarrassment. Eventually, as the intensity and pressure grew, Ryan did give up baseball, and I really couldn't blame him. What should have been an enjoyable experience even for a few more years was no longer fun.

Even his dad added to Ryan's pressure, without realizing it at the time. He would stand there on the sidelines and call out to him, trying to get him to pay attention to the ball. He thought he could "coach" him a bit himself, and help his son be a better player than he was. One day, Ryan was bold enough to have the presence of mind to tell his father how he felt. He said, "Dad, you're embarrassing me." It was a wakeup call for the father. Why *was* he always shouting at him?

Ryan's dad admitted that "it was more for me than it was for him; I wanted him to be something he wasn't. In the end, I was just being loud and he just wanted to have fun." How many of us do the same things when we watch our kids? Just let the coaches do their thing, and let your kids play at their level.

I read an article that stuck with me about reversing those roles. Imagine you're in a situation where your child is watching you play golf, and if you made a bad shot, your kid would run onto the course screaming about what a bad shot it was, and telling you that you should have done it *this* way, and this isn't the way we taught you! It's hard sometimes for parents to realize that what they're doing is negative behavior until someone points it out to them.

I suggest that all parents should identify their motivations before signing a child up for sports. Are the expectations you set up your own, or realistic for your child? There are some kids who enjoy sports and feel a passion for it, but others are just not cut out for the intense competition that may come with it. And of the ones who enjoy it, very few are going to become professionals—so it's important to make sure their goals match yours. If they just want to have fun and get some exercise with their friends, they won't benefit from parents who just want to win, win, win! Pushing kids into roles they're not comfortable with is an inappropriate use of parental power.

Parental Contracts

In response to the trend of parents becoming too aggressive on the sports field, many schools and town leagues now require parents to sign a "spectator agreement" when they register their chil-

SAMPLE SPECTATOR AGREEMENT

The members of my family may attend practices and games, and we agree to the following rules of conduct:

- We will offer encouragement to the players, and refrain from calling out insults or negative comments.

- We will remember that effort is more important than winning, and that sports are meant to be fun for the children.

- We will allow the coach to be the instructor. We will not attempt to coach from the sidelines, or to argue with the coach's instructions.

- We will not step onto the playing field without permission from the coach. We will remain at least ten feet away from the sidelines when watching the game.

- We will not argue or fight with other spectators.

- We will not argue or fight with any officials. If we disagree with the way something was handled, we will approach the coach politely during a break in the game or after the game ends to talk about it.

- We will not use profanity or profane gestures.

- We will not bring any alcohol to the games or practices.

- We will not throw anything onto the field or players' area.

- We will not attempt to distract any of the players or officials, and will not unnecessarily disrupt the game.

- If we see bullying behavior between players or from spectators to players, we will report it to the coach immediately.

We understand that penalties for breaking these rules may include ejection from games and practices on a temporary or permanent basis, at the league's discretion. We understand that the objectives of this league are to teach leadership skills, build teamwork, promote good sportsmanship, improve athletic skills, and provide an enjoyable atmosphere for all players, and we will support those objectives.

X _____

Date _____

dren for sports. Essentially, it says, "We as parents agree to abide by the rules and take responsibility for our own behavior."

The contract doesn't necessarily put an end to the bad behavior, but it should at least cause parents to think twice, and it provides justification in writing for any consequences that may arise from a parent's bad behavior. If a parent's behavior is particularly egregious, the coach or supervising body can bar the parent from attending any further games.

The Coach's View

Bob Wagner, a coach in Rochester who runs SoccerClasses.com, agrees that the biggest bullying issue he sees these days stems from parents. "We find that there are parents who have unattainable expectations for their kids, the coaches, and the referees. They are often verbally abusive to the referee as well as to their own kids. If I see this behavior from parents of the kids I am responsible for, I talk to them individually about their behavior."

The club he works with has become very attuned to the problem, and spends time before the season begins talking to all the parents about appropriate behavior. They're now beginning to do more education, including showing videos about bullying and aggression.

"I try to paint them a picture of what they sound like before it happens, so they can think before they act. Most parents who get carried away are quite embarrassed by their behavior afterwards."

Compared to the numerous parent incidents he recalls, he remembers few kid-on-kid bullying incidents, but says there was one recently between fourteen-year-old girls. The best player on the team was picking on another player, first verbally, and then with a slight shove. He saw this, made her apologize, benched her for the game, and told her mother about the problem. The girl was very unhappy about it at the time, but learned from her actions and has even become an assistant coach since then.

"With all of the training that I do, I strive for discipline from the kids and their parents," he says. "The kids are reflections of their parents, so if the parents are left unchecked, the kids often feed off of their abusive behavior. That is when you start to see the kids play recklessly, and verbally abuse opponents or teammates as well as the referee. I find that if we manage the training environment, we see fewer incidents when we get to game times." For parents, remember this: Your kids may reflect in their actions what your behavior looks like to them. If you see your children acting like bullies, first take a look in the mirror, and ask where they have learned this. This is a big step for any parent who is serious about bullyproofing their child.

Rule Reminders

The more visible the rules are, the better. It's a good idea to have signs posted with simplified versions of the rules around the stands and entrance. Even very simple signs such as "Let's have fun!" and "Please cheer for good effort" can serve as good cues.

It's also a good idea for the coach to send home reminders throughout the season along with any paperwork that needs to be given to parents. The coach should make copies of the spectator agreement so that the parent who signs can bring home additional copies to go over with other family members and friends who may attend games.

If you were never asked to sign an agreement and have not seen rules posted, it's worthwhile to ask the coach or official to make the rules clearer. You may want to bring in the sample spectator agreement, or suggest rules of your own based on what you've seen in the stands.

What's important to remember, though, is that the coach must be the "point person." It's not a good idea for parents to try to approach other parents to tell them their behavior is not acceptable. Unless you know the other parent in question and have a good relationship, it's too risky to try handling the problem yourself. You don't know which parents are going to take it well and which ones will become more aggressive or violent in response. It's best to talk to the coach and ask her to talk to the parent privately.

The same goes for bad behavior from opposing team members. It's not a smart idea for parents to approach kids about their bad behavior, and the kids are much less likely to pay attention to scolding that comes from a parent who holds no authority in the game. If you see kids heckling, shoving, or otherwise bullying, tell your team's coach and have her take it up with the opposing team's coach. Repeatedly, if necessary.

Remember to approach the coach in a calm manner. Bullying the coach is not a good form of role modeling! If you don't get the resolution you want during the game, try approaching the coach again after the game to talk about it, and if that still doesn't work, try writing the coach a note or calling the next day, after the coach has had time to think about it and is no longer in the busy environment of a game.

Training for Coaches

The coach is the director of the whole game, and must be given the authority to deal with all behavior problems that arise. One problem with that, however, is that coaches are often not trained to deal with bullying issues. When bullying behavior is a problem on the field or in the stands, it's a good idea to talk to the coach's supervisor to ask that the coach receive more training to deal with the issue.

The school or league can bring in a professional to speak to the whole team (and parents), or just train the coach one-on-one to better manage the problem. Some schools and leagues also have a "Coach's Code of Conduct" that outlines what's expected of coaches in terms of appropriate behavior, how to handle aggressive parents, how to handle bullying among kids, what is and isn't allowed on the sports field, and so on. You can find a sample of one such contract at http://tinyurl.com/gzs7m.

Signs That a Child Is Being Bullied in Sports

Because children will not always come out and tell you about the problem, watch for these signs that the child may be having trouble with bullies on the sports field:

- Unexplained injuries (bruises, cuts).

- Torn or missing clothing.

- Loss of enthusiasm about the sport.

- Self-esteem diminishes. Uses negative self-talk such as "I suck," "I'm never going to be any good," "I blew it again."

- Makes excuses to skip practices or games: stomachaches, headaches, other pains.

- Gets sensitive to any sort of criticism about the game.

- When you watch games, no one passes him the ball or speaks to him on the sidelines.

- Wants to be alone after games or practices.

- Wants to quit.

If the child wants to quit, try to get to the bottom of the problem before agreeing to it. If it turns out that there's a bullying problem, see if it can be solved—and if so, if the child's interest in playing returns. However, if the child has just genuinely lost interest in the sport, never force the issue. There are plenty of other activities that may be a better match for your child; not everyone is meant to be an athlete and your child may come back to it at a later time.

Depending on your child's demeanor, you may want to approach the subject in a direct manner or an indirect manner. It's usually best to ask easier questions first, such as, "What do you like best about practices? Are there any nice kids on your team?" Then you can transition to questions such as, "How do you rate as a player compared to other kids on the team? Do you ever see kids getting teased? Do you see kids getting picked on and hurt? Does that ever happen to you?"

If you find out that there's a problem, work with the child on a bullyproofing plan, as discussed in chapter 2.

How Jocks Become Bullies

It's a stereotype that athletes are often the school bullies. Of course, not all (or even most) athletes are bullies, but the stereotype exists for a reason.

Athletes are generally stronger than the other kids—tougher, more agile, more intimidating. That in itself gives them an advantage over other kids in the bullying arena, but it goes further than that.

- Athletes are taught to be aggressive, and told that the more aggressive they are, the more likely they are to win.

- Athletes often get preferential treatment at school: they may

THE COACH WITH THE RIGHT APPROACH

Swim coach Poppy Redmond says that kids are not good at understanding other people's feelings, which is why it's important for an adult to explain the impact their behavior has on others. Very often, once children understand that what they're doing is hurtful, they stop.

"I remove the kid from the pool and take her away from where the other kids can hear what we are talking about," she says. "Sitting comfortably, I quietly explain her behavior and its impact in a friendly, caring, conversational tone, and ask her how she thinks this makes the other person feel. The tone is important because a harsh tone will put her on the defensive, and when kids are on the defensive, most of what you say is deflected before it is heard. The child also needs to know that you care—that you know she can do better

have an easier time cutting class, or get passing grades when they really deserved to fail.

- Adults in authority praise athletes, often reinforcing their place at the top of the pecking order.

- Recruiters may treat star athletes like celebrities, spoiling them with gifts and bribes.

It's important to discuss leadership responsibilities with the better athletes. They need to understand that the qualities they have that make them leaders on the sports field are gifts to be used to help people, not to stomp on "weaker" kids.

If you see that athletes at your child's school are hurting other kids and getting special treatment, bring it up with the coach and then the principal—and if he's the one condoning it, bring it to the school board. They must understand that this special treatment of and you are questioning only that one behavioral issue, not her whole person. She needs to know you still believe she is a good and valid person *and* (never *"but"*) there is one change you would like to see. Good coaches and managers know to praise publicly and criticize privately.

"If explaining the outcome of their behavior does not work, then asking them why often does. I use the kids-nagging-their-parents 'why' technique. Why are you doing this, why do you want to do that, why, why, why . . . until they run out of answers. It makes them think about what they are doing and why, and usually they come to their own conclusion that it is not actually achieving the result their subconscious mind thought it would. Then, usually they abandon the behavior and try something else."

bullying athletes enables the most powerful kids to grow superpowers; now not only are they already the toughest kids in school, but they've found out that people in authority favor them, which means they will soon believe (if they don't already) that they can get away with anything. In some cases, they know the principal will just tell the coach to talk to the kids if they've misbehaved in school, and the coach will blow it off.

This is where we see the more egregious behaviors start: kids on sports teams pulling down other kids' pants in front of their peers, sexually harassing girls, stuffing boys' heads in the toilet or into lockers, and so on. They can be this brazen because they believe they have the school officials in the palms of their hands. Sadly, they're often right. But when parents point out the discrepancies to school officials with documentation, it becomes harder for them to continue the preferential treatment. They'll realize parents are on to them!

The "Fab Five"

A high school in Texas made national headlines in early 2007 because of the actions of a small group of cheerleaders, who were accused of terrorizing their fellow classmates, teachers, and coaches, while simultaneously being protected from discipline by the administration. They posted sexually suggestive photos of themselves on MySpace in their cheerleading uniforms, and photos of themselves drinking and smoking, but were still allowed to remain on the squad.

The girls went through four cheerleading coaches in a year. After coach Michaela Ward resigned, the school district hired a lawyer to investigate the problem and write a report. He concluded, based on interviews with seventy students and staff members, that the girls were getting away with terrible behavior that included skipping class, telling off their teachers, flouting school rules, sending sexual text messages . . . and bullying their classmates. To top it off, the mother of one of the girls was the school principal.

On *Good Morning America*, the former cheerleading coach said, "Unfortunately, these girls were given power that any teenager would have completely abused. They were untouchable. They were invincible. The rules did not apply to them. There was no accountability. They knew that I had absolutely no power to discipline."

The principal resigned, and as of this writing, the assistant principal is on paid leave. The fact that so many newspapers and television programs picked up on this story is a testament to the fact that this sort of elite culture is pervasive among teens. At most schools, a similar clique exists—a group of athletes who seem to be "above the law," who can get away with behavior that others can't. And were it not for the fact that the cheerleading coach took her story to the media, perhaps nothing would have changed in this school.

It underlines the need to continually seek out higher-level authority figures if you get nowhere with the first person you turn to. This coach explains a climate of fear among teachers, in which they knew their jobs would be in peril if they tried to discipline any of the "Fab Five." In this case, parents would have had no luck complaining to teachers or the principal. They would have needed to move on to the district level.

Picking Teams

Getting picked last in gym class is such a notoriously damaging experience that it's nearly a cliché. What happens is that a gym teacher picks two team captains, and they take turns picking kids from the class for their team, until they're left with "slim pickings"—usually the kids who are overweight, disabled, uncoordinated, or unpopular. And those kids get to be further marginalized as they stand around uncomfortably, watching the captains' faces contort as they decide who among them is the most undesirable teammate of all.

There's no good reason in the world to let kids pick teams this way. Most gym teachers do it strictly out of habit. That's the way it was done when they were in school, and considering they were probably never picked last, they don't see what's so bad about it. Maybe some of them see it as a way to toughen kids up—that if they don't want to get picked last, they'll improve. Instead, they're mostly just traumatized and spend the games trying to hide as much as possible and not humiliate themselves further by making a bad play.

It's just as simple to pick teams in a random fashion, like having students count off ("One," "Two," "One," "Two") or handing out red pinnies to half the students and blue ones to the other half as they exit the locker room. Or just let the gym teacher or coach pick teams if random picking isn't working between students.

Another creative way to ensure that teams will be about equal in ability is to have one captain pick both teams—she picks both teams from the available kids, then the other captain gets to pick which team she wants to lead. In that way, the one doing the choosing won't make either team obviously better than the other or she's likely to get stuck with the "bad" team. If the captains are rotated each time, this reduces the marginalization of kids because it makes things much fairer.

Call the gym teacher if you find out that your child is feeling bad about the way teams are chosen. Chances are that the teacher may not have thought through what an embarrassing experience it is for the ones chosen last. The goal should be to decrease the opportunities for humiliation in sports.

Locker Room Supervision

Locker rooms are known to be bullying hot spots. If you recall bullying incidents from your own youth, chances are that you can recall at least one incident that happened in the locker room, away from adult supervision. It's a place where girls make fun of other girls' bodies, where boys get into physical fights, where kids steal things out of lockers, and more.

When I was in junior high school, I played on the school basketball team. One of the other team members didn't think I belonged on the team, and after every practice, he would make this known by throwing the ball at my head in the locker room. There was never any adult supervision, and the other kids would just stand around and laugh. It was awful.

My coauthor often received detention for being late to class because she would go to an out-of-the-way bathroom to change her clothes rather than subjecting herself to locker room gossip. After numerous scoldings for being late, she decided to arrive at school wearing her gym clothes and then change out of them at lunchtime.

There should always be supervision in the locker room when kids are in there. If you find that there are locker room problems in your child's school, call the athletic director or principal and explain that there is a bullying issue that needs to be addressed, and that it's important for a teacher or aide to be present in the locker rooms at all times.

Hazing on Sports Teams

Hazing is best known as an activity that happens in college fraternities and sororities, but it can actually happen in any group setting. The kids who promote hazing would say that it helps build the togetherness of a group. However, hazing is a ritual that's meant to embarrass, demean, or endanger new members of the group, and is usually carried out by the oldest members of the group. Hazing can be part of school tradition, or a rite of passage that all kids who join the group experience. Hazing is a form of bullying and has no place in athletics.

Hazing occurs because kids want to feel powerful and achieve status and position through their power. There are lots of other ways to model leadership and success in front of younger athletes. It takes a good coach and athletic directors to challenge hazing rituals and take a stand from the very beginning of every season and throughout the year and promote success in athletics through good leadership. Hazing continues to happen unless the leadership comes up with strategies to stop it, and the most successful one besides creating awareness for the athletes is to help them feel empathy. Athletes should be encouraged to care about how their teammates feel. A supportive coach has a chance to change any hurtful behavior that may have preceded her. Coaches who make these discussions mandatory, and offer brainstorming for their students, have a chance to create new opportunities for group cohesion in their athletic team.

A boy recently told me that when he joined the lacrosse team as a high school freshmen, he and the other freshmen members were forced to stand up on cafeteria tables and sing "The Itsy-Bitsy Spider." What's so amazing about that is that it happened just two years ago. Now, knowing all we do about bullying and the need for supervision, cafeteria aides allowed this to happen without comment? The boy is going to be a senior this year, and as such, it's his turn to haze the freshmen. He's very conflicted about it because he hated the experience; he found it humiliating to have to stand up in front of his peers and sing a children's song. But it's a team tradition, and he's feeling pressured to carry it on. Does this really prove an athlete's worth? Did the coaches and athletic team at this school really not know it existed? Or did they tacitly accept this ritual as a nonproblem?

As hazing events go, of course, singing children's songs isn't the worst of the bunch. In 2003, at a preseason football training camp in Mepham, New York, four varsity students sodomized several junior varsity boys with pine cones, broomsticks, and golf balls covered in mineral ice. The coaches were asleep in another cabin. It was reported that most of the squad was aware of the attacks, but none of them reported what happened. A victim finally came forward more than a week after the assault only because he needed surgery.

Hazing often involves binge drinking or using drugs; often has a sexual component (mooning, streaking, masturbating in front of people); and may include tasks such as doing an upperclassman's homework for him, dressing in women's clothing, saying embarrassing things to girls, or stealing items from a convenience store. Some of you may be smiling or crying when reading about this now, depending on your experiences. Just because hazing is something steeped in tradition doesn't make it right.

Most people realize that the criminal acts are problematic, but oftentimes, hazing incidents are overlooked in that "boys will be boys" way. When they're overlooked, teammates see that as an official sanction, and they are likely to continue pushing the line into more and more extreme hazing behavior. It often isn't until a student dies of alcohol poisoning or comes forward with sexual assault charges that school officials wake up and realize that there is hazing at their school.

Bring any such incidents to the attention of the coach, and the principal if there's a safety issue involved. (If there are criminal acts involved, call the police as well.) Make sure they promise confidentiality, and that they promise to specifically address hazing incidents with their sports teams. Prevention here is the key. Good coaches are open to discussing hazing right up front, come out against it, and encourage good problem solving and brainstorming with their athletes to identify newer and better ways for building a solid, cohesive team.

Tragic Endings

Bullying in the youth sports arena has made headlines sometimes for particularly horrible reasons, such as the time in July
2005 when a thirteen-year-old boy was convicted of murdering a
fifteen-year-old boy with a baseball bat.[24] The older boy had teased
the younger boy about losing a game.

The boys were in line at a snack bar, surrounded by other kids
and parents after the baseball game, when it happened. Witnesses
said that the younger boy—a pitcher for the Palmdale Pony
League—got angry about the teasing, and when the older boy
shoved him, the younger boy grabbed an aluminum bat out of an
athletic bag and swung twice: at the older boy's legs and head,
killing him.

At least one witness, a coach, testified that the older boy had a
reputation for being a bully. This is likely a case of a tormented child
coming to the end of his rope because of ongoing bullying. Luckily,
that doesn't happen often. Most children, no matter how much bullying they endure, will not strike out violently and put anyone else's
life in danger. It's far more likely for a bullied child to withdraw and
walk away than to get into a confrontation. But there's always the
possibility, as cases like the Columbine and Virginia Tech shootings
hauntingly remind us.

What happens in those cases is that the child is no longer thinking about himself. He doesn't care what happens to him at that
moment. All he wants is to get back at his tormentors, and he's
blind to everything else around him. It happens most often when
he thinks no one is listening to him, no one is stepping up to help
him, no one cares, and no one is going to stop the bully any
other way.

It's important to note that people said this was very out of character for the younger boy. People characterized him as nice, a good student, and respectful of authority. But it's certainly possible that warning signs were missed. Picking up a bat and hitting someone in the head isn't normally something that a child does based on one-time teasing in a snack line. Normally, an act like that is building in the child's mind for some time. He's fantasizing about revenge, thinking about how nice it would be to finally show the bully that he's not weak. This is no different from the targets we saw in school who need bullyproofing strategies. Targets need to learn to deal with their own feelings so they don't act out.

The only way you're going to find out if your child is having feelings like this is to ask. "How are you getting along with your teammates? Is there anyone on the team or the opposing teams who you have a problem with? Does anyone on your team get teased, or picked on constantly? Does that ever happen to you?"

If you already know your child has a problem with a particular other child or group of children, address it to see how serious the problem is. "Does it make you very angry when they do that? Do you feel like you can control your anger? What can we do to work on this problem so you don't need to feel this way anymore?"

As much as we want to eliminate all instances of bullying, it's not realistic to expect that. Therefore, it's still very important to teach children how to manage their emotions and stay calm even when they're feeling hurt, angry, or embarrassed. Depending on how severely it affects the child, it may be something you can work on with her as a parent, or it may require the help of a counselor, too.

The most important concept to convey is the "So what?" response. It may not feel natural to the child the first couple of times, but kids often find it liberating once they've done it.

When a kid on an opposing team says, "You guys suck! Ha, ha, you lost," a good reaction would be, "So we sucked! You're right. We lost. Big deal." Where is the bully going to go after that? There's nothing to argue with.

The more the child tries to defend or get angry in return, the more it prolongs the taunting and the more likely it is to escalate. Much better to agree with the bully, shrug it off, and take away the power of those words. It's not the first instinct of many bullied kids, but it's a skill that can be learned and put to good use.

"You're right! Whatever you say! Cool." These kinds of comments show the bully that there's no meltdown likely to occur here, which means it's no fun to keep up the teasing. A bullyproof child is no fun to attack.

Team Heroes

When I talk to sports teams about bullying, I encourage kids to become "team heroes." The idea is that the team that pulls together has a better chance of winning. Even on professional teams, one team may have the best talent, but they won't win games unless they work together as a unit. The way to become a unit is to develop a team spirit, and that means standing up for each other and not putting each other down.

When one team member picks on another, the bystanders on the team have to pay attention. A "team hero" is the type of kid who will stand up and say, "Let it go. He did his best. Leave him alone." That way, camaraderie stays solid and it becomes clear that picking on team members isn't tolerated by the test of the team. Negative talk can be squashed on the spot if team members are willing to stand up for each other, even when someone "lost the game" for them, or made a bad play.

A Good Sport

Sports should be a stress-free activity for kids, giving them time to unwind, have fun with friends, and get fit. No child should ever be forced to play sports, or to stay in a sport they no longer enjoy, because a parent insists. And they should not be expected to tolerate bullying behaviors on the sports field that they wouldn't be expected to tolerate in school or in other activities. It's your responsibility as a parent to attain a safe environment for your child, emotionally and physically, so don't be afraid to speak up as often as needed if you spot foul play. However, don't stand up in a way that demonstrates your own foul play!

SIX

Bullying at Camp

BULLYPROOFING THE BUNK

Summer camp can be a wonderful experience for kids, providing them with a unique opportunity to make friends and learn new skills and tools for life. Camp staff provides the nurture, reinforcement, support, and most important, the opportunity for children to be whatever and whoever they are without the pressure from academics. Kids go to camp to try out new activities, develop new friends, and share living space with other kids around the clock.

An adolescent I work with shared something that explains the way many kids feel about camp: "In school, I'm considered really smart and stereotyped in a way I can't ever change, so kids can't really see who I am, but as soon as I go to camp, I can be anything I want to be, and no one cares if I am smart or anything else. It's the one time of year I look forward to being free."

For kids who are low on the social ladder at school, it can provide a new chance to find refuge from the school bully and thrive in a different environment. This can only be successful if a camp is knowledgeable about bullying, takes it seriously, and utilizes lots of strategies to prevent and manage it. I have made it my mission in life to reduce bullying, especially in summer camp, when kids are more open to be themselves and want a break to enjoy their life without the pressure they feel throughout the year.

However, for some children, camp can be a nightmare if they experience bullying and they don't feel safe when they are away from home. Bullying thrives in unstructured atmospheres where supervision may feel looser, and camps can provide the perfect atmosphere for bullying to flourish, unfortunately. Kids generally have a lot more free time and possibilities to mingle with each other in camp, as opposed to school. In school, bullying happens about four times more often on the playground versus in the classroom, and camp can be like one giant playground. For example, bullying in camp occurs when supervision is lean: on the way to activities, during shower time, during free play, and when kids are in their cabins and counselors are not readily visible.

Whether your child attends day camp or sleepaway camp, there are precautions you should take and ways to deal with bullying situations that arise.

The Counselors

How many times do we hear children speak about their summer being "great" because of their mentors, the counselors? What makes a great summer are the relationships kids make. Besides friends, they want to feel accepted, loved, cared for, and connected to their staff. From my own work in the bullying arena, one can see where there's an obvious overriding problem: Most of the staff are teenagers and young adults. The average age of a counselor is nineteen to twenty-two, but in many camps, high school students are hired for these jobs, even if it is in the counselor-in-training format. The potential problem that brings is that these counselors are not very far removed from the prime bullying years in their own lives. They don't necessarily yet have any insight about how to handle bullies, and they're still worried about their own popularity and social standing.

Kids tend to know the social hierarchy in any group situation, whether that's at school, camp, or elsewhere. They figure out pretty quickly who's at the top of the ladder, who's in the middle, and who's on the bottom. So do counselors, even if they don't say it out loud, and counselors tend to align themselves with the kids at the top of the ladder. This is a normal human trait, wanting to connect with popularity. However, for a counselor, this issue has severe consequences, especially if it involves a child who is not a popular kid.

Lana's Quest for Recognition

One thirty-year-old woman recalls her day camp experience this way: "There were two counselors assigned to each group. At the end of every camp day, they gave out a 'Camper of the Day' award, and announced a reason—'Danielle is our Camper of the Day because she hit a homerun in softball for the first time today.' It was a certificate with a gold seal and the kid's name written in colorful bubble letters, and every day, I hoped with all my heart to be the special Camper of the Day. It was an eight-week program, so you can figure it this way: Five days a week for eight weeks is forty days. There were about twenty girls in my group, so each girl should have been Camper of the Day twice throughout the summer, by simple odds.

"Well, I was a quiet kid, not athletic, not particularly pretty, and fearful. But I was very good at crafts and I participated in all the plays. I kept hoping that the counselors would one day notice and say, 'Lana is the Camper of the Day because she sewed a beautiful teddy bear,' or 'because she did a great job singing in the camp play.' But that's not what happened."

Instead, Lana remembers, there were two girls the counselors obviously favored. They were pretty, outspoken, confident, and athletic—and tended to bully Lana and her only friend at camp. They were not the world's worst bullies, but they knew they had power and enjoyed making others feel small. On a special "movie day," each girl got a bag of popcorn, and the popular girls would "ask" Lana to share hers with them—then they'd pass it around to their friends and give her back the empty bag. They'd tell Lana there was no room at their lunch table, even though there were obviously seats open. They'd purposely hit tennis balls over the fence when forced to play with her, then make her go retrieve them while they laughed with each other.

The counselors awarded these girls with "Camper of the Day" awards regularly. The prettier one got the award five times, her friend got it four times, and twice, they got it together! This is something Lana remembers *twenty-one years later*, because it bothered her so much that the meanest girls were so obviously favored. The counselors would announce their reasons: "Sherri is Camper of the Day because she's so cute" or "Sherri and Tracy are both Camper of the Day today because they make such a great team, like Mutt and Jeff."

Maybe the counselors liked them so much because they were such great swimmers, Lana surmised. She was terrified of swimming, and hated the feeling of putting her head under water, but decided to make it her goal to learn to dive that summer because, well, the counselors would have to notice that, right? On the day of her first dive, Lana was sure she would finally get recognized, but instead, someone else got the award for nothing in particular.

One time, Lana's friend got the award. She looked sheepish as she accepted it, knowing that the counselors were basically compelled to give it to her because she'd won some kind of campwide tournament that day. At the end of the eight weeks, Lana was the only one who had never received an award.

"It's such a silly thing, but I was devastated. It was as if the counselors had directly aligned themselves with the bullies and made sure never to acknowledge that I had any worth, no matter how hard I tried to excel at something. I remember all the anticipation I had on that last day of camp, thinking, 'Please let this be my day.' And when they gave the final certificates to the two bullies, I wanted to cry. I probably did, once I got home. And I begged my parents not to make me go back to camp the next year."

Lana's counselors may not have been aware of the bullying behavior, but because of the obvious favoritism, it would have felt impossible for Lana or her friend to speak up to the counselors about it. They didn't think they'd be believed, or worse—that they'd be believed, but that the counselors would side with the bullies anyway.

Training Counselors

Lana's story emphasizes why it's so important to train counselors properly, and teach them how to create a good environment that doesn't further exaggerate the social hierarchy already in place. Note that it wasn't the bullying that made Lana want to leave camp; it was the counselors' implied *approval* of that bullying.

Staff members need to be trained about what to look out for and how to handle bullying. Nearly all camps have an orientation period when counselors learn about their duties; rather than tacking on a quick mention of bullying in the middle of talks about schedules and sleeping arrangements, it needs to be covered in detail, with plenty of realistic examples. This can be accomplished primarily through role-playing—having counselors act out the parts of kids who are name-calling, shoving other kids, doing something meant to humiliate, excluding someone, and so on.

First, they should be shown ways it could be handled incorrectly (for example, telling the target to stop being a baby, or ignoring the situation, or joining in, or telling the kids to fight it out on their own) and then they should be encouraged to model the "right" way, without ridicule or harsh judgment from leaders or other counselors. If directors encourage them to take risks with these role-plays, they're more likely to remember the behaviors and try them out with their campers.

Then the counselors can role-play these scenarios with the kids in their cabin, or the director can use this as an opportunity to do a camper set of role-plays in a larger group the first few nights of camp to set the structure on how the camp identifies and manages bullying behavior. This sends a strong message to both campers and staff and begins the season with a clear definition of what acceptable and unacceptable behavior is.

Counselors should also be taught to reward "prosocial" behavior. They should have talks with kids about teamwork, and helping kids who are having a hard time, and including new campers in their social circles. When a counselor sees acts of kindness among campers, she should reinforce the good behavior with praise. If a counselor sees antisocial behavior, it needs to be addressed immediately and definitively.

When I give talks at camps, I ask the returning counselors to talk about their experiences with bullies. Their stories help the new counselors learn what to expect and what to watch out for. One counselor told about an athletic fourteen-year-old boy who demanded to be the first in the shower every day, and would taunt

BULLY PREVENTION SHOULD BE MORE THAN JUST ORIENTATION TRAINING

Staff may feel bombarded with orientation information. They take in so much information that they may become overloaded with material and expectations. Ideally, bully prevention begins with leadership training during the year, training of counselor staff during orientation week, and ongoing discussions with staff throughout the summer. The camp leaders need to include questions during their daily meetings with staff about kids who are teased, excluded, or have difficulty with friendships. Staff must remain vigilant all summer with bully prevention or bullies will find the place where aggression will go unnoticed. Counselors take bully prevention seriously when leadership staff makes it a priority in their meetings with counselors.

other boys about their sexuality if they dared try to challenge his authority. When this story was told, some returning counselors shared ways to prevent it from happening again. It puts counselors on the same page and teaches them how to use their authority effectively.

Practical jokes are long-standing camp traditions—toothpaste on the toilet seat, running someone's underwear up a flagpole, putting lipstick on a boy while he sleeps—and counselors need to go over the differences between just kidding around among friends versus intentional humiliation of a targeted child.

Counselors are taught to have regular check-ins with the camp director or other senior staff members to go over any incidents of possible bullying and how they were handled. What a counselor may have seen as an anomaly may be a problem also spotted by the nurse and the sports director.

If they hear hurtful talk, counselors should jump in and defend

Similarly, camp staff has to be vigilant and talk to their campers about these issues in ongoing ways. Regularly, on the way to or from activities, counselors should ask their campers positive questions to begin a conversation. "What do you like most about your day? What activities do you really enjoy?" Then they can move on to harder questions: "Do you ever notice anyone being teased, picked on, or excluded? Does that ever happen to you?" When counselors do this and assure confidentiality with their campers, they build trust, which is at the core of a trusting relationship and successful bully prevention. Campers see these discussions with their counselors as natural and normal when done consistently.

the target. If a group of girls make fun of a camper's clothing or hair, the counselor needs to say something like, "I think Eileen's hair is beautiful." If they try to keep a kid out of an activity, the counselor needs to step in and make sure the kid is included and not picked on. Counselors need to be vigilant about jumping in when they hear gossip, or any negative talk about other campers or even other counselors. When counselors jump into camper situations and say, "Hey, what's going on here?" or "Hey, what's up with that?" or "We don't talk about anyone behind their back" or "How would you feel if someone was saying that about you right now behind your back?" counselors see that their behavior has impact. This kind of training helps counselors define who they are as role models and gives them the power to stop bullying. More important, it shows campers who's in charge and what they can and can't get away with.

I'm a big believer in having counselors who manage bullying

situations with their peers and their campers be given leadership positions as mentors for their peers. This shows others how valued this kind of behavior is for the camp.

Counselors are kids' substitute parents, and they need to understand what that responsibility entails; it's their job to ensure each child's emotional and physical safety, and to be accessible and open enough for children to feel safe reporting concerns. Children need to trust that their concerns will be heard and acted upon by the authority figure they're counting on.

Questions to Ask the Camp Broker or Director

Many parents go through a "camp broker" to select a camp. This is much like a college advisor, who helps match high schoolers to appropriate colleges. Whether you use a broker or not, here are the questions to ask up front before deciding on a summer camp. You can ask the broker or the director:

1. What is the camp director's knowledge of bullying?

2. Is there a written bullying policy I can read?

3. What kind of staff training is done, and how long does the training last?

4. What are staff responsibilities when it comes to dealing with bullying behavior?

5. Who trains the staff about bullying?

6. What procedures do they use if a bullying incident occurs?

7. What are the consequences if bullying is discovered?

8. If you find out a child is being bullied, do you alert the child's parents?

9. Are campers given any training on identifying the various types of bullying in camp?

10. Are there any specific methods the camp uses to reduce the incidence in bullying? For example, how do you deal with generally less supervised areas in camp?

Of course, all brokers and directors are going to say the "right thing" because they want their camps to sound good. They will all tell you they handle bullying and that they may have a "zero tolerance" policy. That isn't necessarily the "right" answer because it doesn't tell you anything. Therefore, as a parent, avoid the simple questions that yield little help, such as "Do you train the staff to watch out for bullying?" Every director will say yes, but that may really mean, "On the first day of camp, we tell the counselors, 'Bullying is bad. And swim class starts at eleven.'"

Try to find out an actual name: Who is training these counselors? Is it a professional psychologist or other qualified instructor? You can jot down the name and try Googling it later to see if the person is known in the bullying field.

When you ask what kind of training is done and how long it lasts, ideally you'll want to hear that training includes role-playing and lasts for at least half a day during counselor orientation, with follow-ups throughout the season.

Not all camps have written policies yet, but even if they don't, they should have established protocol that they follow based on the type and severity of bullying. What you don't want to hear is, "We decide each case one by one as it comes up," or "Sometimes we tell the bully to apologize, sometimes we make the bully sit alone during activities . . ." Instead, ask for a specific hierarchy. What happens when a kid calls someone nasty names? What if someone is caught stealing? What happens when a kid punches another kid? Or sexually harasses someone? What happens when a kid does any of these things repeatedly?

Successful camps have consistent policies and consequences. As in any area of life, of course, cases are considered individually to some degree, but there should be specific consequences that are the "norm" for specific actions.

What Do the Counselors See?

I became involved with summer camps as a bullying coach because a camp director called to talk about bullying incidents he'd experienced over the summer with some kids he thought he knew well. I hadn't thought much about bullying in the context of camps before that, but I knew that bullying can become a problem anywhere kids congregate, so I decided to find out just how much of a problem it was in camps.

According to the directors I surveyed, bullying is one of the top three reasons children don't return to camp the following year. So I have been collecting surveys to try to learn more about what counselors see with regard to bullying, and what they experience themselves. The data I'm about to share with you was collected during orientation week in the beginning of the summer of 2005. More than one thousand counselors from twelve camps answered my multiple-choice questions.

I surveyed staff about their observations of bullying behavior, and divided their responses based on who was answering: a male or a female staff member. In general, these were overnight camps where female counselors are in charge of girls, and male counselors are in charge of boys.

Here is what they reported:

Camper Behavior

Did you observe any of these types of bullying behavior between campers last summer?

	Female	Male
Teasing, name-calling	92%	92%
Verbal threats	59%	75%
Gossiping or rumors	96%	88%
Exclusion or cliques	96%	85%
Embarrassment in front of others	81%	87%
Kicking, pushing, hitting	60%	79%
Stealing of personal things	48%	51%

These data show that most staff recognized bullying behavior among campers. Most male and female staff noticed verbal teasing and name-calling between campers. More male staff saw verbal threatening behavior among their boys. However, almost all female staff observed gossiping, rumors, exclusion, and clique behavior in their female campers, as well as a high percentage of their kids embarrassing girls in front of others. Most male staff also reported a high percentage of their campers embarrassing boys in front of other boys, but more male staff report observing a higher percentage of physical aggression among their boy campers as compared to female staff.

One obvious conclusion is that both female and male staff observe and acknowledge that there's a significant amount of bullying behavior in their campers, and that it's relational and verbal more often than physical. This is similar to statistics in schools.

Staff Behavior

I then surveyed the returning staff about the bullying that occurs with each other, and the percentage of staff that experienced this.

Did you observe any of the following types of bullying between counselors last summer?

	Female	Male
Teasing, name-calling	53%	59%
Verbal threats	26%	40%
Gossiping or rumors	86%	74%
Exclusion or cliques	86%	66%
Embarrassment in front of others	55%	46%
Kicking, pushing, hitting	17%	24%
Stealing of personal things	29%	26%

These data reveal that the staff themselves see a significant amount of bullying behavior with each other. Most female staff experience gossiping, rumors, exclusion, and clique behavior. Two-thirds of male staff experienced the same thing—even though that's usually assumed to be female behavior. Teasing, name-calling, and embarrassment in front of others is noticed by approximately half of all staff. Physical bullying is limited to one out of six females, and one out of four males. Stealing of personal things was observed by approximately 25 percent of both male and female staff. What conclusion can we reach? The bullying behaviors experienced by campers also occur within the camp staff. These behaviors are seen as fairly commonplace among the counselors, and the staff needs to identify these behaviors in themselves if they are to reduce them and role-model appropriate behaviors to their campers.

Statistics like these made me think how "natural" this bullying behavior was, so I thought, "Let me collect some data when counselors first get together during orientation, even before the campers come."

Staff Behavior During Orientation

Have you seen any of your camp staff this summer during orientation do the following?

	Females	Males
Teasing, name-calling	30%	35%
Verbal threats	5%	8%
Gossiping or rumors	63%	49%
Exclusion or cliques	63%	44%
Embarrassment in front of others	24%	24%
Kicking, pushing, hitting	6%	8%
Stealing of personal things	2%	2%

This reveals that *within a few days* of first meeting each other, camp staff shows some significant bullying behavior among themselves. Staff may accept this behavior as part of interacting with each other to fit in, but behind the scenes, these behaviors may create unhappiness and distress. The prevalence of exclusion and embarrassment in front of others can be quite daunting to some. The lines of behavior and what is deemed appropriate or inappropriate are difficult to manage when staff experiences these behaviors so quickly within the first few days of interaction before campers arrive for the summer. Obviously, these behaviors increase over the summer, as seen by the increased percentages in the previous chart, but you can see how quickly these behaviors take root.

We cannot assume that the counselors are aware of this behavior in themselves, or the impact it has on others. If they are not aware of their own behavior, how can they change it in their campers? That's why it needs to be a significant part of counselor training before camp starts. I have made it my mission to train as many people as possible to teach them how to be aware of bullying behavior in others and themselves so they can understand how they can best manage bullying. This is most successful when staff can see their own behavior in action. Ask camp directors if the staff bully training they provide covers staff behavior among themselves.

Types of Camp Bullying

When I ask counselors about specific bullying incidents they see in their campers, they run the gamut from the same sort of teasing, exclusion, and physical bullying you might find in school to some really exclusive behaviors more specific to camp.

Younger girls do "tenting": they put a sheet up on the bed and invite only certain "select" girls into their club. Girls may make a comment about another girl's looks and clothes and make her feel that no boy will like her. Girls may read another girl's diary and make it "public" to the camp. They may talk about other girls' breasts and body hair in ways that shame and humiliate them. I've heard of girls replacing shampoo with other fluids that didn't belong in that shampoo bottle.

Boys can be equally cruel, and they run the gamut in terms of how they bully each other. Boys certainly get physical with each other, but they have learned how to be cruel and do this in ways that are verbal and through exclusion. I've heard about younger boys stealing each other's possessions and money, destroying property that was meaningful to a camper, and humiliating and being shameful about boys' body parts in front of others. How about the bucket of water thrown on a boy, or exposing him when in the shower? Teens get into the "you can't play cards with us" exclusion, or push kids away when they attempt to join a conversation. Some pranks can be pretty humiliating. There are many stories about boys moving kids out of the cabin when they're sleeping, and moving all their personal property, too. I've also heard of boys who "de-pants" each other in front of others, and especially girls.

The important thing I want to share about the bully horror stories is that things are changing and generally these stories happen less often. I seriously suggest to parents to find a camp that is accredited by the American Camp Association (ACA). All accredited camps have access to bullyproofing materials that I have provided, in addition to lots of other great resources. Accredited camps have much more exposure to the kinds of information they need to provide emotional and physical safety to all children.

Camp directors have heard me say that, with extreme forms of bullying, there are no second chances. Kids should not be entitled to stay in camp after torturing someone in such a severe manner.

By far, the most common form of bullying in camp, among both boys and girls, is exclusion (relational bullying). Because camp is almost purely social—as opposed to school, which is more academic—a child who doesn't fit in socially is going to have a terrible summer. In many camps, preteen and teen girls who don't appeal to the boys are seen as useless, and can be made to feel like they're never going to have boyfriends and move up the social ladder. This can crush a girl's self-confidence for when she goes back to school, too. Boys who are not athletic or funny or handsome may also be excluded. This manifests in many ways: kids are left out from sports games they play, or aren't invited to sit with the other kids on someone's bed in the cabin or mess hall, or the other kids get ready and leave someone behind.

With these types of bullying, there is a chance for reconciliation and growth, if the bullies accept the consequences for their actions and show empathy for the target. This goes back to how a camp director manages bullying incidents. Kids who bully need to show some acceptance of responsibility and remorse for their behavior, and empathy for their target, if they are to stop their behavior and reduce their own bullying. When you ask your camp director about consequences for bullying, this is what you hope he or she will tell you.

The Returning Bully

The classic scenario is that a camper who's been coming to the same camp every summer for at least a couple of years may become the "Big Bully," feeling the power and the "right" because of his status on the social ladder, taking it upon himself to intimidate the newest, easiest targets. Just like being the new kid in school, being the new kid at camp is a challenge.

It's important not to let bullies become entrenched. The longer they get away with their power trips, the worse the bullying gets. They learn that adults don't notice or don't act, and they come to believe that they're untouchable. They find great hiding spots behind cabins, in bathrooms, during less supervised activities, where they can threaten other kids or physically hurt them.

Some camps deal with this by never letting groups get too exclusive. Instead of allowing kids to order themselves in the cabins, cafeteria, sports teams, and so on, counselors can assign different groups to different activities. What this does is allow campers to trust that the camp values lots of social connection, and fosters this among their campers. A suspected bullying clique can be seated apart from one another and scheduled separately. New, shy kids can be linked with friendly returning campers.

Although it is not possible to prevent kids from being with their friends, and even bullying cliques, it creates a culture where diversity is valued, and acceptance of others is part of a camp's mission. I think it is important for parents to ask their camp how they deal with cliques and groupings that may be exclusionary. A camp director who knows these problems exist will have a plan that provides lots of opportunity for kids to mix and not isolate each other.

Unlike schools, camps have no legal responsibility to keep a child in the program. There is obviously a financial motive to keep as many children as possible, but it should be easier to have a bully expelled from camp than it is to have a child expelled from school. If camp directors are wise, they'll realize that getting rid of a bullying camper will likely save them from losing several other campers, who may not return if they have a lousy summer because they're targets. Over the years I have been providing training to summer camps, I have made it clear to management that a bullying kid costs them more in lost campers and a loss of trust that they can't well afford. I see a real change in the willingness of camp directors to do the right thing when it comes to sending a kid home when her repeated bullying behavior was not fixed by discipline and consequences.

Sometimes, kids don't even realize that their camp traditions are scary to newcomers. A few summers ago, I dealt with a group of young teen boys who were friends from previous years in camp. They were used to a sort of hazing ritual, where the newer campers would get tormented for the first couple of weeks of camp.

That year, the camp staff had taken a hard-line stance and said that any such behavior would not be tolerated, and that kids engaging in hazing could be thrown out of camp. Well, these kids didn't understand what the big deal was. They'd always played pranks before, and didn't see the harm in it. So when they had a new kid in their cabin, they ignored the instructions and engaged in the "fun" they had planned. After he fell asleep, they'd cover him in Vaseline and baby powder, take his things and hide them outside the cabin, make up insulting nicknames for him, and other embarrassing deeds.

The boy tried hard to take it for the first ten days or so, but he came to a point where he just broke, and called home to say he wanted to leave. When the staff found out about it, they sent the bullying boys home for a week. The targeted boy didn't want that; he felt he would be even more targeted if the boys were thrown out because of him. He had already made up his mind that he was leaving. He was too humiliated and convinced that he didn't fit in.

During the week, the camp director required that the bullying boys see me. I quickly realized that these were not "bad" boys; they had leadership skills and empathy, but had seen their power grow over the years and hadn't stopped to consider that their pranks and teasing might really hurt someone. In their minds, this was "normal" for camp and they had earned their status by being the older boys. They showed remorse, which is the key to deciding whether or not a bully can learn from the incident and return to camp. They even wanted to talk to the targeted boy to ask him to change his mind, but he refused.

That was a sad situation, but it made an impact on the camp. The boys gave a very public apology in front of the entire camp when they returned, explaining what they had done wrong and how they planned to be more inclusive in the future. For the boys who did the bullying, being sent home for a week showed them that the directors were serious about the pranks and bullying this year. The boys had time to reflect on their behavior and do the right thing.

Before Camp Starts

With sleepaway camps, the trouble often starts before camp even begins—kids will e-mail each other about bunk selections, and start gossiping about who they're going to exclude. Has the packet of information you've received from a prospective camp alerted you to these issues?

I urge camp directors to send letters home to parents to ask them to monitor these kinds of activities. Are there campers who are being excluded from camp reunions? Are there instant messages flying back and forth about how they're going to beat up So-and-So? Are there postings about camp counselors or campers on MySpace that are derogatory or negative? I urge camp directors to ask parents to let them know if their kids are involved in negative or exclusionary e-mails that might shift their kids from wanting to return to camp. Since the Internet is fast becoming the primary method of our kids' communication, you have to talk to them about what they see online from other campers or staff. The only

BULLYING POLICY

This is a sample of a written bullying policy I've developed for the American Camp Association, using a fictitious camp's name.

Bullying is when one or more people exclude, tease, taunt, gossip, hit, kick, or put down another person with the intent to hurt another. Bullying happens when a person or group of people want to have power over another and use their power to get their way, at the expense of someone else. Bullying can also happen through cyberspace: through the use of e-mails, text messaging, instant messaging, and other less direct methods. This type of bullying can also lead to persons being hurt during or between the camp seasons, and be especially hurtful when persons are targeted with meanness and exclusion.

At Camp RespectU, bullying is inexcusable, and we have a firm policy against all types of bullying. Our Camp philosophy is based on our mission

way parents can know if their child may be excluded is to ask their children:

1. Have you heard about any get-togethers from camp where you weren't asked to go?

2. Have you received any e-mails that made you feel left out?

3. Has anyone been saying bad things about you?

4. Has anyone said anything private about you to others that made you feel bad?

Parents need to be made aware of the camp's policies on bullying. What will happen if their child is implicated in a bullying incident? Will the camp director always call parents if there's a problem?

statement, which ensures that every camper has the opportunity to acquire skills, knowledge, friendships, and life experiences. We work together as a team to ensure that they gain self-confidence, make new friends, and go home with great memories.

Unfortunately, persons who are bullied may not have the same potential to get the most out of their camp experience. Our leadership addresses all incidents of bullying seriously and trains staff to promote communication with their staff and their campers so both staff and campers will be comfortable alerting us to any problems during their camp experience and between camp seasons. Every person has the right to expect to have the best possible experience at camp, and by working together as a team to identify and manage bullying, we can help ensure that all campers and staff have a great summer at Camp RespectU.

What system is in place to report bullying? Are there bunk rules the parents should be aware of?

It's a good idea to encourage parents to go over the camp's expectations and rules with their children, to make sure that kids are aware that camp isn't a free-for-all where they can behave badly, and to make sure that kids who are prone to be targets are aware of who they can talk to and what to do if they don't feel safe.

If your child has been bullied in school, or may have had a lot of experience in the bullying arena, either as a target or a bully, and you don't want the camp to know about this, you are making a mistake. Camp directors can treat this information confidentially and let camp staff know which campers need a little extra "watching," without anyone else knowing. A camp director who is sensitive about this gives your child more protection and the possibility for a better summer.

The Director's Role

Role modeling starts at the top. When you evaluate a camp for your child, try to see how the director talks about or acts with staff members. If the director acts like a bully toward the staff or you when you ask questions, what do you think the odds are that this is going to be a positive environment for your child?

Think of your own experiences with bosses or teachers. Certainly, you've had some who made you feel safe asking questions, and others who ruled by intimidation. You wouldn't dare ask a question or reveal a vulnerability, or you'd worry that you'd get yelled at, ridiculed, fired, downgraded, and so on. Counselors who are treated this way can be afraid to ask for advice about bullying situations, and afraid to admit that they don't know how to role-model the right behaviors. Counselor staffs, like campers, need to have continual reinforcement and training about where the "acceptable versus unacceptable" line may be.

Eagle Eyes

When I talk to counselors, I ask them to picture themselves as eagles instead of ostriches. If they can soar above the landscape, they can get a clear view of what's happening below. The eagle's perspective can give them a lot of control over what happens in camp.

As a parent, you want to know not only that there's a high number of counselors to supervise the campers, but also that the staff is vigilant, and that kids won't be left unwatched during "free time."

One young man tells this about his day camp experience when he was about seven or eight years old: "We had some free time, so one of the kids in my group asked if I wanted to play one-on-one soccer. I did, and scored the first goal. A boy called me over and asked me if I could keep a secret. 'Sure,' I said. Then he punched me in the stomach, hard.

"I felt sick. 'Remember, you can't tell anyone,' the boy said. I nodded weakly and he kicked me and walked away."

That afternoon at home, his mom knew something was wrong. Rob was too quiet. Finally, he burst into tears and told her about the boy who had punched him. Against his wishes, she called the camp and told the counselor. The counselor, in turn, got the two boys together and asked if it was true, and asked the other boy to apologize.

Rob got extremely lucky for one reason alone: The other boy wasn't an entrenched bully. He was testing his bullying prowess, and once he was called on it, he didn't do it again. He grumbled a little about how Rob wasn't supposed to tell, but he didn't cause any further problems. However, that's not how it should be handled with a more established bully.

Counselors need to be taught about confidentiality, just like teachers. If I were to advise in a situation like this, I would have told the counselor not to involve the target at all. Instead, I would have asked him to be more vigilant and try to observe bullying behaviors himself (why were the two boys unsupervised when they went off to play soccer?), have a talk with the whole group about bullying and the need for reporting if they see someone being bullied, and issue reminders about what's acceptable and unacceptable. During this talk, he can emphasize that punching and kicking are not acceptable, and that if anyone sees this sort of behavior, he wants to know about it and that he would make sure that the information was confidential. This builds trust, which is a key component to helping campers feel safe.

Just like the confidential reporting box for classrooms, there can and should be a confidential box where campers can notify staff members about bullying concerns, away from the bunk if it's an overnight camp. If there is such a thing, then the counselor could have told the bullying boy that there were a few reports from campers who had witnessed his bullying behavior. That takes the blame off the target. I tell camps to put these boxes in the infirmary, where kids can safely report without having to worry about being seen.

Otherwise, the target's summer may be over. Getting known as a tattletale (and worse—a tattletale who has to have his mom fight his battles for him) is one of the worst possible things a kid can experience. It almost always leads to exclusion and verbal torment, even if not an escalation of physical bullying.

The staff needs to be on the lookout for the campers who may be toward the bottom of the social ladder in each bunk. In an average camp group, there's a top 20 percent, a middle 60 percent, and a bottom 20 percent of kids on the social ladder. While the top and middle ones may get bullied occasionally, they can normally handle these situations themselves. But the ones on the bottom need the most intervention. Staff should watch for campers who walk alone to activities or the dining hall, who show up first to activities (because they have no one to spend free time with, and prefer to be in the organized environment where staff is present) or last (because they had to wait behind the other kids to take a shower or eat, or because they were hiding to get changed). It should be obvious that some kids possess less developed social skills than most. If your child is one of those kids, don't be afraid or ashamed to tell the camp about it. The more they know about your child and his experiences, the better adapted they will be to watch and prevent bullying. A good camp director will treat this information confidentially, and use his camp staff to be aware of your child's vulnerabilities, so they can be quick to act if a problem comes up.

It's imperative that staffers link these children with other campers to help them make friends and feel connected. Having one good friend at camp can reduce bullying incidents by 50 percent or more.

CAMPER REFLECTION FORM

After consequences for bullying have been completed and after the emotion has subsided, I encourage counselors to use a form such as this one to help bullies (or potential bullies) reflect on their behavior and commit to making a change. This is a form I've adapted from Stan Davis's book Schools Where Everyone Belongs *(Research Press, 2005).*

Campers have less incentive to try to blame others or get out of responsibility at this point and can reflect better on their behavior and what they did wrong. If they do not take responsibility for their actions, counselors should work with them to find better answers and to feel how their actions affect others.

Name: _____   Date: _____

What did you do wrong? Start with the word "I" and don't blame anyone else for the actions you took. (At this point, how you handled yourself is the only thing that matters.)

What was wrong with the choice of using this behavior? (What cues did you see or hear from them to know when you hurt them? Were there words or facial expressions or emotions they showed you?)

What were you trying to achieve by your actions? (Did you want to feel powerful, get some attention, or be left alone? Were you trying to have fun at someone else's expense, or were you mad about something else?)

continues . . .

> Next time this happens, what can you do to solve it without hurting some-one else? Give three ways to do this.
>
> What can you do now to make this right for the other person in an honest and meaningful way?

It's also helpful for staff to find something that targeted kids can feel good about within themselves, and to reinforce it in front of other campers. Counselors who give campers social value can change a summer for them.

Hierarchy of Consequences

Not all bullying incidents are created equal, which is why there should be different consequences based on the type and severity of the problem. And as much as possible, counselors should outline those consequences right up front on the first day of camp, when talking about the cabin rules and what's expected and what's unacceptable. The camp director can send a letter to parents in advance about the overall camp rules, so parents can go over the basics with their children before they arrive, and the counselor's talk with campers can serve as a reminder of the basics and more specific guidelines.

Sometimes, talking it out, filling out the camper reflection form, and apologizing are enough to solve the problem.

For more serious infractions, counselors may use "time-outs," when a bully is not allowed to participate in an activity for a period of time. Or the bully may be separated from her friends, or moved to a different cabin if bullying behavior is not managed after the first incident.

A serious and effective consequence is having kids call home themselves to tell their parents what they've done. Kids don't want to have egg on their faces, to have to let their parents know that they've done something bad enough to merit a trip to the office to call home. Once the child is finished, the director or other leader should pick up the phone and explain to the parent that further behavior like this won't be tolerated, and that the child is in danger of being sent home if it continues.

Then, for the worst behavior, bullies can be sent home either for limited periods of time, or for the rest of the summer.

Greetings from Camp

At one point, the only real way kids at sleepaway camp communicated with their parents was by postal letter. If the kids complained of homesickness or problems with other campers, by the time the parents received the letter, the problem might have been resolved. Nowadays, many camps allow the use of e-mail and cell phones, so kids have instant access to vent their spleens to their parents. This is a good and a bad thing.

Emotions run high among kids, particularly when they're away from home in an unfamiliar setting. The natural pressures of trying to fit in with a new group, coupled with the fear of being away from home, can create high drama—but usually also foster growth and end up being a positive experience. What they feel right now may be totally different ten minutes from now. So in a way, I prefer more limited communication, with a time delay. Otherwise, it's too easy to make snap decisions to pull a child out of camp before allowing the camp staff time to intervene or allowing the child to deal with the experience. As a parent, you don't want your emotions to dictate your behavior and cause you to call the camp and bully the director in the heat of the moment. But a director can know that your child has reported a problem and he needs to check it out.

Of course, if you get a letter or call from your child that sounds desperate, or feels like your child is in an unsafe situation (physically or emotionally), or if there's a pattern to these kinds of letters, you'll need to call the camp immediately and tell the leadership staff to find out what's going on. Make sure you have all the specific information possible: names of the kids, locations of incidents, dates and times, counselors' names, specific words and actions against your child, and any evidence you have (e-mails, photos, etc.).

Tell them that you'll expect within a day a return call and explanation of the situation and what they'll do to resolve it, and that you expect confidentiality—no running back to the bully to report everything you've said, which would only make your child feel embarrassed and more vulnerable. Instead, ask the director what his plan is. Look for a response that includes the following possibilities: he will talk to the staff and ask them to be more attentive to the situation, to keep a closer eye on your child and the bully or bullies, and to talk to all the campers in that group about bullying—what's acceptable, what's unacceptable, what to report, what the consequences are, and how to be a good bystander.

When a director takes this stand, the situation should improve. If a director provides little or no reassurance, you can certainly encourage her (without bullying her) to do the very things mentioned above and get back to you when she has taken some action.

Camp staff should let parents know they're dealing with the problem, and the parents should expect to hear from the child within a couple of days that things have settled down. Otherwise, if the problem continues or escalates, it's appropriate to talk to the director again, and let her know that you are still concerned about your child's safety and happiness. Ask the director for more information on how your child is doing and what she plans to institute to ensure that your child is feeling safe. When all else fails and you do not feel that your concerns are being addressed, it is then appropriate to let the director know that you intend to take your child out of camp and expect a pro-rated refund if physical and emotional safety issues are not being managed. This expectation is not feasible if your child is asked to leave camp because of bullying.

Be mindful of your tone during conversations like this. Often, parents try to "bully" the camp staff, and this tends to make the staff dig their heels in and feel less empathy toward the child. You want to emphasize that your child feels unsafe or unaccepted at the camp, and that the camp has a duty to protect your child. But you want to do this without becoming shrill or threatening.

Your child also needs to feel that she has allies among the camp staff and doesn't need to come to you with every problem. It's important for counselors and leadership staff to communicate with the child to let her know she can come to them confidentially and talk about problems that may come up. When children feel they have an adult ally that they can speak with confidentially, it usually allays the situation.

In a day camp setting, parents are still able to mediate problems similarly to the way they'd handle school bullying. If you pick up the child at camp, you can just walk right into the office to talk about

ACTING OUT IN RETALIATION

Sometimes, the target is the one who ends up getting punished for bad behavior. That was the case with Jason, a boy I worked with who was a bit eccentric and socially awkward. Unlike the boys in his bunk, Jason wasn't into soccer and rowboats and softball. His hobbies were things like watching horse racing and listening to country music. The other boys were pretty brutal to him, calling him names and making him feel like he was unacceptable.

What made it worse was that Jason was overreactive. He was prone to anger and dramatic reactions, and would say goofy things that he thought were clever insults. Obviously, this just fueled the bullying. It was a pressure cooker scenario because he was with these boys twenty-four hours a day. So, just two weeks into camp, he's the one who got sent home because he

any problems the child has mentioned, and be more active in helping with a bullyproofing plan. And if a child needs to take a day or two away from camp until a plan is developed, that's feasible.

Tell the director that you would like to be notified of any and all bullying incidents and any progress that is made, good or bad. Let the director know that you'd like the two of you to be on the same team and strengthen each other's efforts. To do this, you can reinforce positive behavior in your child with specific praise such as, "Your counselor told me you controlled your temper when another child pushed you. That really helped the other campers not to get in a fight."

Counselors Shouldn't Become Crutches

There's a tricky line for counselors to walk. On one hand, staff who stay back or do not respond consistently set the tone that the negative behavior will be tolerated. On the other, if they step in began breaking other kids' things, stealing, and fighting with the kids who bullied him. In his mind, he was trying to get sent home; he thought it would be better to be thrown out than to quit.

We had to work on the Power Contest and how he played that game. When we first met, he was really traumatized by these boys at camp, but he had to learn over time to let things go and to be less reactive. We practiced and reviewed his body language and comments in taunting situations. I got him to let go of the goofy responses he was giving in favor of straightforward responses, and I reinforced his calm behavior. That was very helpful as he went back to school, and I just heard from his mother that he's having a successful experience at a new camp this year.

every time a kid teases another kid, those kids will never learn how to solve problems themselves.

Vulnerable kids often look to counselors as de facto parents, and just as a sister and brother may spend half the day saying, "Mom! She touched me!" so may campers expect this kind of constant intervention from counselors. It's usually not a good idea for a counselor to do too much coddling, however.

When possible, the "oversensitive" child needs to be taught that teasing is no big deal, and that he or she can act cool about it and become less of a target. Counselors should never engage in put-downs ("stop being a wimp," "don't be a baby," "if you'd stop annoying them, they'd leave you alone"), but they can find more positive ways to let targeted children know that it's time to work on their own social skills.

For example, if a camper tells me, "He said I'm a loser," I'd say, "So what? At times, I'm a loser, you're a loser, and everyone's a loser, too. You won't feel like a loser when you don't get mad about that."

You can try to have the child put things in perspective by asking how much it bothered her. A lot, a medium amount, or a little? If it's a little or a medium amount, then she can probably just ignore it and think about something else. If it's a lot, then she can talk to the counselor about it if she needs help solving the problem. I encourage counselors in my trainings to help kids put these things in perspective through the power game role-plays we do. Teaching a kid to feel like a true winner by learning how to socially manage other kids can be the real success for kids in camp and teaches them a set of tools they can take home forever.

Camp Reunions and Events

Often, campers will want to get together throughout the year for parties or informal socializing. Just as with classmates' birthday parties, the appropriate rule here is: half or all and nothing in between.

If a child wants to have a party, he can either invite everyone from the bunk, or half (or less) of the kids from the bunk. It is not appropriate to have a party and leave just a couple of kids out. Then it's exclusionary. It's not easy for a parent to enforce this, but it's a strong lesson. Parents typically don't think about invitations this way, but you really have to if you want to set the tone about doing the right thing. Encouraging your kid to be inclusive, especially about camp, sets a tone that carries through to the next year, and reinforces what camps encourage: inclusiveness where all kids get a chance to have a good time. This is more difficult with older kids who want to make their own decisions, but encourage your kids not to be exclusionary.

If your child is the one being left out of events like this, it's appropriate to call the camp director and ask if he or she would

BOSSY MISS BRENDA

I worked with a nine-year-old girl who had the tables turned on her. She was considered the bully at camp, and she didn't realize it. She thought she was pretty cool her first year of camp, but when she was ready to return the next summer, she found out that the girls had asked not to be put in her cabin, and some said they hoped she wouldn't come back at all. She was devastated and didn't understand how the girls couldn't like her.

She had a strong entitlement mentality, and expected to always get her way. I had to show her how her bossiness was bothering the other girls, and how she was crossing the line into selfish behavior rather than nice, inclusive behavior. With the help of her parents, I steered her to show more concern for her peers and what they wanted, too, and she was able to make a positive turnaround. When kids can reach out beyond themselves, and set a tone for inclusion that is consistent, they can lose their "mean girl" status.

speak to the parents about this. It's not in "camp spirit" to leave kids out of activities that are camp-related, even if they happen during the school year. Obviously, a camp director cannot force a parent to do the "right thing," but it's worth a try. When a camp director calls a parent who allowed exclusion, it sets the value of the camp message even more strongly. The parent may not even realize that someone is being excluded, or may not have thought about how it might hurt the child.

Camp Lessons

Camp should always be an enjoyable experience for kids, not a terrifying one. If your kid is coming home from day camp upset, fearful, grouchy, insecure, withdrawn from you and friends, and talking about wanting to quit, or calling home from resident camp with somatic complaints like stomachaches, headaches, nightmares or feeling distressed, and sounding distant, afraid, or sad, make sure to ask questions to find out if bullying is to blame. Don't assume that the camp staff doesn't care. It may well be that they're not aware of the problem, and would actively work to fix it if they knew what was happening.

As parents, give the camp and your child a chance to turn it around, because this can instill a better sense of self-confidence in your child. It's far better to go through a rough patch and learn to manage it, trust in others, and have your child feel resilient than to leave in fear and learn nothing but avoidance. And if your child can learn to move past bullying in the camp environment, he'll be more socially confident and less likely to be bullied in other environments. The best thing about camp is it may be that place where your children can feel most connected, make long-term friends, and create who they want to be. I can't tell you how many kids tell me that is what camp is for them.

SEVEN

Bullying in the Cyberworld

The Internet is the new bathroom wall.

Whereas years ago, kids would write their anonymous gossip on bathroom walls ("For a good time, call . . . ," "Kerri slept with Darren," "George is a fat pig"), now they've found a way to send their nastiness to a much wider audience.

The newest and potentially most dangerous form of bullying, "cyberbullying," is growing so fast, it is proving difficult for researchers and therapists to keep up. In fact, as we were preparing this chapter for publication, a new study just reported that cyberbullying among teens and preteens has increased by 50 percent in the last five years.[25] Just as people have quickly adapted to communicating with each other through e-mail, text messaging, message boards, and blogs, bullies have likewise lost no time in using these modes to bully and terrorize. We as parents need to learn the language of the Internet so we can discuss these issues with our children.

Parents who don't know what to look for online, or how to prepare their children to communicate on the Internet appropriately, are opening a door to potential problems. So let's look at the issue and what you can do about it.

The Newest Set of Bullies

What makes cyberbullying so difficult to manage and control is that it is often anonymous and indirect, and because of that, it expands the pool of potential bullies by enabling large groups of kids to launch a coordinated bully attack without ever facing their target. It is much easier for children to be mean when there is no direct contact. Kids will type things on the computer they never could say in person, and this medium makes it much easier to be impulsive and press the "send" key without considering the consequences.

Cyberbullying also generates unpredictable power configurations, creating a new set of bullies who would never have otherwise bullied someone. Kids who are more "nerdy" and get picked on or shunned in school are often the ones who are the most computer savvy, and can exact their revenge online.

Cyberbullying is also a bit more common among girls than boys. Girls tend toward indirect bullying, and this fits right into the model because they don't have to face the person they're tormenting.

Types of Cyberbullying

There are various types of abuse that can happen online and by cell phone. Here are some of the types that crop up most frequently:

- **Websites created to harass.** It's simple to create a website, and many providers offer web space free, so there have been several instances where kids have built websites dedicated to harassing a peer. One such website was called "Kill Kylie Incorporated," accusing the student of being gay and threatening her life. It took police nine months to catch the kids who were behind this, and Kylie transferred to another school.[26]

- **Impersonation.** A student impersonates another student and sends out messages purportedly from that person. In one noted case, someone discovered the password for a thirteen-year-old girl's website and made it look like she said horrible things about each of her classmates. But more often, impersonation doesn't even require actual hacking into an account—the kids may just use a screen name that appears to come from the targeted child.

- **Gossip groups.** Message boards, blogs, MySpace pages, and e-mail groups can be used for nefarious purposes, and often are. Kids may group together and discuss kids they don't like, under fake names or anonymously, like an online "slam book." There are even sites where people can vote on the school's biggest slut, most hated student, most boring student, and so on. The comments are online for anyone to read, and can remain online forever, serving as a painful reminder for the target.

- **Photo and video postings.** On sites such as YouTube.com, kids can upload embarrassing videos they've made of others or managed to intercept, or display attacks they've made on other kids. Kids can often record video clips on their cell phones and post them online. These may include images they've recorded in the locker room, at a party, on the bus, and so on. The images can be doctored using a photo-editing program, too. In one case, a boy recorded himself singing a song to a girl he had a crush on, and it was disseminated across the Internet to humiliate him. How impressive are these videos to our children? Google thought they were pretty hot: They bought YouTube.com for $1.65 billion.

- **Direct bullying.** Of course, kids do threaten and torment other kids directly by e-mail, instant messages, and text messages. A child may be surfing around online when a message pops up: "Everyone at school hates you," or "Watch your back tomorrow, because my friends and I are going to kill you." Most of the time, these types of messages are delivered by people with fake names, or screen names created for just this purpose. A message sent to a girl named Heather might come from the screen name "HeatherIsASlut." Kids may get these messages at home, or on their cell phones or computers while at school.

- **Unwanted registrations.** If the bully knows the target's e-mail address, he can register the target for all kinds of unwanted e-mail. For example, a bully might subscribe to sexual newsletters under the target's name and e-mail address.

How Common Is It?

Fight Crime: Invest in Kids is a nonprofit organization of more than three thousand police chiefs, sheriffs, prosecutors, other law enforcement leaders, and violence survivors. In 2006, they conducted a nationwide study about cyberbullying to find out how prevalent it is, where it's happening, and what kids are doing about it. They defined cyberbullying as "the use of electronic devices and information, such as e-mail, instant messaging (IM), text messages, mobile phones, pagers and websites, to send or post cruel or harmful messages or images about an individual or a group."

Their research group conducted telephone interviews with 1,000 kids, breaking them into two groups: "preteens" (ages 6–11) and "teens" (ages 12–17). These were the key findings of the study:

- One-third of all teens and one-sixth of preteens reported that they have had mean, threatening, or embarrassing things said about them online.

- Ten percent of the teens and four percent of the younger children were threatened online with physical harm.

- Sixteen percent of the teens and preteens who were targets told no one about it. About half of children ages 6–11 told their parents. Only 30 percent of teens told their parents.

- Preteens were as likely to receive harmful messages at school (45 percent) as at home (44 percent). Older children received 30 percent of harmful messages at school and 70 percent at home.

I also conducted a study in the summer of 2006. I surveyed 1,222 young adults, ages 18–22, to ask about their cyberbullying experiences. Here's what they told me:

Percentage of Young Adults
Who've Experienced Cyberbullying

I asked if they'd been targets of cyberbullying through each of the following methods. Below are the percentages who answered yes to each question.

Method	Male	Female
E-mail	7%	14%
Instant Messaging	17%	30%
—impersonating by IM	15%	17%
Blogs	8%	8%
Text Messaging	6%	9%
MySpace or Xanga	3%	4%
Facebook	2%	4%
Camera Phone	1%	1%

Then I asked if they'd cyberbullied other people, and here's how they answered:

Method	Male	Female
E-mail	6%	5%
Instant Messaging	14%	15%
—impersonating by IM	10%	10%
Blogs	2%	4%
Text Messaging	6%	3%
MySpace or Xanga	2%	1%
Facebook	2%	2%
Camera Phone	1%	1%

CYBERBULLYING CAN LEAD TO SUICIDE

Ryan Halligan was a thirteen-year-old boy from Poughkeepsie, New York, who was a special education student until the fifth grade (it was then determined that he no longer needed special education services). Fifth grade was when the bullying started: a boy and his friends picked on Ryan because of his academic weakness and poor physical coordination. His parents advised him to ignore the kids, and brought him to see a therapist to boost his self-esteem.

But the problem worsened in Ryan's seventh grade year, the same year he developed an interest in computers and began spending lots of time chatting online. He broke down crying and asked his parents to move so he could go to a new school, or to homeschool him. He wouldn't let them tell the school principal (he said it would only get worse; he'd seen it happen to other kids). Finally, they agreed that he should learn to defend himself, so he and his father began practicing kickboxing.

He did wind up getting into one fight with the bully, and things seemed to improve after that. It wasn't until after Ryan hanged himself that his father was able to find out how bad things were for his son in the months leading up to his death.

John Halligan was able to open his son's account and read all the instant messages he had written and received for the past three months. What he found there was shocking. A popular girl pretended to be attracted to him, then humiliated him by showing his messages to other girls and telling him she'd never go out with such a loser. The original bully had floated an unrelenting rumor that Ryan was gay, and a pseudonymous student would send him sexual come-ons to perpetuate the harassment. A boy Ryan's parents had never met chatted with Ryan online and encouraged him to kill himself. And Ryan visited websites about suicide.

Although his parents did realize that Ryan was depressed and knew of his troubles, they believed it was "teen angst" and that he'd get past it. John now spends a great deal of time campaigning for antibullying legislation and speaking to student and parent groups. He urges parents to closely monitor their children's online activities, and is an advocate of computer monitoring software.

An Ounce of Prevention

There are steps you can take to reduce your child's risk of being bullied or bullying others online.

First, allowing a child to have his own computer comes with parental responsibility. If you are the kind of parent who wants to learn the language of the Internet, ask your children about their online friendships, and make sure your children are being open with you, then the bedroom computer use will not hurt you. But if you are the kind of parent who doesn't have these kinds of discussions with your kids, then *do not* allow the child to have a computer in his or her bedroom or other private area. Remember that kids will test limits as they are get older and the computer may be a main source of testing. If you suspect any problems, keep the computer(s) in open areas such as living rooms or dens, where you can walk in freely.

Strongly remind children that they are not to give out their full names or any personal information online, including their phone number, address, town, school name, photo, and so on.

If they're going to participate in chat rooms, message boards, e-mail discussion groups, and the like, tell them not to write anything that they wouldn't want to see on a giant billboard in front of the school the following day. You can also tell them to think about writing e-mails as if they were writing their grandparent. Don't say anything online that you wouldn't say to your grandparent in person. This helps them gain a perspective on respect and the language they use online. Remind them that even if they think they're just talking to a few friends, anything that's written online can be copied and posted on websites or forwarded around to thousands of people.

Tell them that if someone sends them an instant message or

e-mail, and they don't know who the person is, *do not respond no matter what*—even if the person seems friendly. Kids use fake names to fish for information to use against their targets.

Sometimes kids set "away" messages on their instant message program that clue others into where they are or how to reach them, such as giving their cell phone number. Make sure your child doesn't do this or provide any personal information online so others can see it. Anyone, including bullies and predators, can send a message to that screen name and get the automatic "Away" message.

Tell them to pick passwords that are difficult to guess: not their birthdates, or their favorite band, or their favorite hobby, or their pet's name, or anything like that. Pick a combination of letters and numbers, and if it has to be written down, write it in a hidden place. Some kids trade passwords with each other as a sign of trust or friendship; tell them not to do this under any circumstances! Kids' friendships are too fragile to be relied upon in this way. A child's best friend today might break into her e-mail and forward her private thoughts all around the school next week.

However, passwords should not be private from *you*. Parents have differing opinions on where the line is between respecting their children's privacy and being a concerned parent, but Ryan Halligan's father suggests that protection trumps privacy. If your child is unwilling to trust you with his password if you promise him that it will only be used in extreme situations, then you probably need to be more careful with his Internet use.

Do Unto Others

While you're teaching your child how to avoid being a target, remember, too, to address the other end of the equation. Keeping in mind that children who are targeted in other areas of life (school, camp, etc.) can switch roles and become the bullies online, make sure you go over what's acceptable and not acceptable behavior.

One reporter, studying cyberbullying, was shocked when a top honors student—quiet and well behaved—admitted to sending death threats online. He had no intention of ever following through on any of his threats, so he thought it was okay. It gave him a sense of power. But not only was it not morally okay, it also could have landed him in a heap of trouble if police had gotten involved.

Make sure your child knows that it's never okay to threaten anyone online, make fun of others, post embarrassing photos, impersonate others, sign people up for spam, forward private e-mails to other people (even other friends—who might one day become enemies), engage in "three-way chats" where one party isn't aware that there's someone else silently watching, and so on. Also, even if your child isn't one of the ringleaders, remind him not to vote on the sites meant to judge the kids in school who are the ugliest, fattest, stupidest, sluttiest, and so on. Remind him that it would feel awful if it were done to him, and that it's important to be a "good bystander," meaning that it's never okay to support the bullies by encouraging their hurtful behaviors.

Snooping Versus Helping

There's a significant difference between the parent who reads all his child's e-mails and private messages even when no problem is suspected, and the one who scans for suspicious e-mail addresses from people outside the child's known circle of friends, or who has already tried getting answers from the child about why he's depressed or withdrawn and looks for clues online.

Petra, now a mother herself, remembers that her parents spied on her for no good reason, and it almost broke their relationship

QUESTIONS TO ASK YOUR CHILD ABOUT CYBERBULLYING

 Depending on the child's age, you'll need to alter these questions to be a bit more age-appropriate, but here are the basics to ask about:

- How do you usually spend your time online?

- Which websites do you visit?

- Do you have a blog? Do you have a profile online? Do you have pictures of yourself online anywhere? Would you show me?

- Do you use instant messaging programs? Who do you talk to? Do you ever get messages from people you don't know? What do you do?

- Do you know how to block people from sending you messages?

- Do you participate on any message boards or chat rooms? Where? What is your screen name?

- Have you ever given out information such as what school you go to, how old you are, what town you live in, or what you look like?

- Do you know what cyberbullying is? Have you ever seen anyone get cyberbullied? Have you ever participated? Has it ever happened to you?

- Have you seen websites where people make fun of kids in your school?

- Have you ever given anyone your passwords to your e-mail or any online account?

- Have you ever received e-mails, instant messages, or text messages that were threatening or upsetting to you? (If so, what did you do about it?)

- How would you respond if someone were bothering you online?

- Show me who's on your buddy list. Tell me who each of these people are.

- Do you know that you should save any e-mails, instant messages, or text messages a bully sends, even if you decide not to read them?

- Do you know that you can always come to me if you have a problem online?

apart permanently. She was an honor roll student who had a nice circle of trustworthy friends, had never been in any trouble, and was not depressed. Yet she was scolded for feelings she had revealed only in her diary, and later found out that her parents were recording all her phone calls.

This is inexcusable behavior done either out of paranoia or just a blatant disregard for privacy. If the child has given you no reason to spy, *don't do it*. If you do have reason to spy—you believe your child's emotional or physical safety is at stake—talk about it first. Give the child every possible opportunity to tell you what's happening. Kids tend to clam up about bullying incidents anyway, but cyberbullying perhaps even more so. They fear that you'll take away the computer or make them stop using the features they want to use (chat, instant messaging, MySpace, etc.) if they tell you about a problem. You can reassure your child that you know the computer is important and that you have no intention of taking it away.

If you decide to monitor, then do it in the least invasive manner possible. Skip past the chatty conversations with known friends and family. Resist the urge to find out who your son has a crush on, or whether your daughter has gone past "second base." Be there to learn only the necessary information: Is someone bullying your child online? Is your child bullying someone else? Is your child talking about depression or suicide? These are the kinds of things you need to know. The rest is snooping, and it's more likely to ruin your relationship with your child than to help.

Contracts for Computer Use

At http://kids.getnetwise.org/tools/toolscontracts, you'll find several sample contracts you can use or modify however you like. These contracts cover the ground rules you'll set up with your child, and you can have your child sign and date the contract.

But fair is fair; there's also a parent agreement here: www
.cyberangels.org/parent.pdf. Among other things, it says you promise not to snoop for no good reason.

Smart Teens Doing Dumb Things

While we were working on this chapter, we spotted a perfect
example of a teen using the Internet inappropriately. A thirteen-
year-old girl showed up on my coauthor's message board asking
for mentors to "lead the way" and critique her romance novel—
and offering up her e-mail address. The girl used her real first name
and photo and continually brought up her age (even using a calen-
dar ticker to count down to her fourteenth birthday), and over the
period of a month or so, began revealing more and more information about herself.

She didn't like her public school and said she'd been bullied her
whole life. She wanted to "hook up" with a boy named Louis. She
was a gymnast. She wanted to talk to rape survivors because she
was writing a novel about rape. She was a size 2, and very petite.
Then came the topper: She told us she was transferring to a new
school, and *showed us the link* to the school—along with details
about her schedule. So now anyone who was lurking knew exactly
where to find this girl, and even what classes she'd be in on any
given day.

Yet when the issue of online safety came up, this same girl
specifically bragged about how smart she was and how she'd never
fall prey to a predator.

But in reality, she was making herself a very easy target for both
adult sexual predators and cyberbullies. It wouldn't have been
hard for a classmate to track her down on this website and read
very personal information about her (and what she thinks of her

classmates), which could then be forwarded around and used against her. And if she had been bullied at her old school, now those bullies knew where her new school was, and could contact her new classmates to spread rumors about her.

Social Networking Sites and Blogs

If your child is ten or older, it's likely that he has an online journal of some sort, and you probably know nothing about it. Now, that's not immediate cause for freaking out, but it is cause for awareness.

There are different sorts of "social networking sites," with MySpace.com leading the pack by far. Other popular sites of this kind include Friendster.com, Xanga.com, and Facebook.com, and by the time this book is published, there will surely be others. These are sites where kids (and adults) can sign up for free web space and use it to put up photos, create a profile, keep an online diary, write messages back and forth with their friends, visit real-time chat rooms, and meet new people. Cyberspace has created a new social life for kids, so we can't avoid believing this will be part of our children's experience. We just need to be better adapted to talk about it with them and deal with it.

Many kids use these sites responsibly and have no trouble. Others set themselves up for problems. Before doing anything else, have a conversation with your child about it: Ask if she has an account on any of these sites, or if she keeps any kind of blog or online journal. If you want your child to keep an open relationship with you, it's important to ask the questions before snooping around.

MySpace

To start an account on MySpace, kids must state that they are at least fourteen years old. This, of course, is no guarantee that they actually *are* fourteen or older; there's no age verification process. But if MySpace discovers that a child is under fourteen, they say they will delete the account.

If your child says she doesn't have an account, but you want to verify, go to http://search.myspace.com and type in search terms: Try your child's name, e-mail address, or school.

Parents' first reactions are often along these lines:

"OH MY GOD! HE HAS A MYSPACE ACCOUNT! HE'S GOING TO GET KIDNAPPED AND MURDERED! I HAVE TO DELETE THIS ACCOUNT NOW!"

But if your child is older than fourteen, resist the urge to delete the account without talking to your child. Just having a profile on MySpace is not necessarily asking for trouble; it depends on what's there and what the child is using the site for. If you find out that the teen is giving out personal information, posting provocative photos, teasing other kids, or chatting with strangers, it's time for a "tough love" talk and a firmer set of guidelines.

Deleting the account will probably just anger your teen, and she'll likely create a new account and do a better job of keeping it hidden from you (using it at friends' houses, school, or while you're not home). Better is to give specific examples of kids who've gotten into trouble because of the same types of behaviors, and explaining why you won't accept it.

MySpace has privacy options your child should use. Once logged in, click "Account Settings," then next to "Privacy Settings," click "Change Settings." There, it will allow you to make changes, such as hiding the profile from view of anyone who isn't on your child's "friends" list, and removing the graphic that signals when your child is online.

If, however, your child is underage or your rules aren't working, MySpace offers tips for deleting your child's account here: www1.myspace.com/misc/RemovingChildProfiles.html. You can also block access to MySpace, or any other website, by following the instructions here: www.theparentsedge.com/block_myspace.html.

Some parents have a different way of keeping an eye on things: They get their own MySpace accounts, and require that their kids put them on their "friends" list, which automatically lets the parent see the child's profile, photos, blog, and anything she writes on her web page.

One thing to keep in mind is that even if your child is not doing anything "wrong"—just having innocent chats with friends and posting a few snapshots that are not risqué—she still runs the risk of having someone make nasty comments. For some kids, having a stranger type "You're ugly" in their comments can send them straight into depression.

Blocking the Bullies

In nearly all cases, the proper way for a child to respond to a cyberbully is not to respond at all. If bullies have fun driving their targets to the brink of a meltdown in person, they get positively giddy when they get to do it behind the cloak of anonymity. Tell your child not to respond when he gets e-mails, instant messages, or text messages from people he doesn't know, or from bullies he does know. This applies even if the bully is telling lies, taunting him, swearing at him, asking questions . . . It's very difficult for a child to show restraint and ignore these sorts of messages, but any kind of response is just going to encourage the bully to continue. If he feels up to it, he can write back one time to say simply, "Stop writing to me. I'm not interested."

After that, he can never write back again, not even to repeat that message. Instead, he should print or save the bully's messages to show you. (Depending on the content of the message, you may wish to contact the school, the Internet provider, or the police—more on that in a minute.)

Sometimes, the solution is as simple as putting a block on the bully's address. Each e-mail provider has a different method for blocking e-mails, but it's generally a simple process of just inputting an e-mail address into a form. If it's not readily apparent to you, call the Internet Service Provider or search their help files and ask.

You can do the same with most messaging programs. AOL's Instant Messenger has several privacy options; if you click "Preferences," then "Privacy," you can choose who can contact your child. One option is to block specific users, but since kids change screen names frequently when they're trying to cause trouble, this can be hard to keep up with. Instead, if your child has had trouble with bullies, I suggest using the "Allow Only Users on my Buddy List" option. Then your child fills in the Buddy List with her friends' screen names, and those are the only people who can send her instant messages. She can always add people as she likes, or take people off the list.

The other possibility is to have your child change e-mail addresses, screen names, or cell phone numbers (depending on which avenue the bully is using), giving out the new information only to very trusted friends and family.

Tracing Cyberbullies

One significant problem with anonymous or pseudonymous bullying online is that it's very difficult to track down the person or people responsible, and police are unlikely to take a real interest unless there are death threats or other physical threats involved.

However, there are steps you can take to improve the odds of tracing the bullies and/or getting the offending material removed from the Web.

Self-Googling

One way to find out if your child is being targeted online is to do a Google search for your child's name, in quotation marks. So if your child is Sally Kinsworth, you'd go to www.google.com and type in "Sally Kinsworth." If your child has an unusual name, you shouldn't have to wade through too many irrelevant links. Common names are harder to search for effectively. You can try adding your state, child's school, or other search words to narrow it down. Then search for your child's e-mail address and any screen names you're aware of.

This won't show you every possible offense online, but it's a good start, and can clue you in to the sites where your child posts messages.

Forward E-mails to
the Bully's E-mail Provider

The e-mail provider is generally whatever comes after the @ sign. For example, if the bully is sending messages from someone@aol.com, the e-mail provider is AOL (www.aol.com). If it's someone@hotmail.com, the e-mail provider is Hotmail (www .hotmail.com). Visit the website of the e-mail provider and look around for a "report abuse" link. If it's not readily apparent, look for a TOS (Terms of Service) link, an AUP (Acceptable Use Policy) link, a contact link, or an "About Us" link. Often, the e-mail address to report abuse is abuse@(name of e-mail provider).com. If you find no other address, try that one as a default.

You'll need to know how to include the full headers on e-mail. This is the information that shows where the e-mail came from. To learn how to show full headers, which depends on your e-mail provider, visit www.haltabusektd.org/help/headers.

Once you have this information, you'll need to paste it into a message along with the forwarded abusive messages (or send them as attachments, depending on the instructions for the e-mail provider you're contacting). Explain your complaint, the ages of the children involved, and any pertinent details.

Be aware that e-mail providers will almost never tell you what steps they've taken, nor will they divulge the identity of their customers without a subpoena. (You can have police or a lawyer obtain a subpoena if necessary.) However, they may send a warning, or suspend the user's account for a limited time or permanently. Be aware that kids often just register a new account, but it may slow down the behavior.

Contact the Website

If there are bullying comments about your child on a website, contact the webmaster, site owner, or customer service contact at the website. If you're looking at a long URL, you'll want to erase anything that comes after the domain name (the homepage, which is everything that comes before the first slash in a long address). Let's use a page on my own website as an example:

www.bullycoach.com/programs/school/default.htm

If you found something nasty about your child written on that page, you'll want to go to the homepage of the site to find an appropriate person to contact. The homepage is the first part of the website address (up to the .com, .net, .org, .biz, or other extension). In this case, the homepage is www.bullycoach.com. You'll go there and find a "contact us" link, which you can then use to write to the person who runs the site (in this case, me) to point out the offensive material and what you want done about it.

You'll need to give the exact website address where the offensive material appears, and quote what it says. Often, all it takes is a simple note, such as, "My son is twelve years old, and is being cyberbullied. His bullies have posted hateful messages on your website at www.bullycoach.com/programs/school/default.htm, including this comment by 'hford': 'George is a loser and a fag' and this comment by 'cobra': 'Everyone hates him and he should just die.' Please remove this offensive material promptly. I would appreciate if these users are not allowed to post further harassment of my son on your website."

Allow twenty-four hours for a response; if there is none, try again—and copy it to another e-mail address at the site, if you find one. If you used the "abuse" e-mail address before, try the customer service one now, or the "webmaster," or the general contact address. You might also find a phone number, fax, and mailing address. If your e-mail does not elicit a fast response, try one of these other methods.

Contact the Website's Hosting Company

You'd need to approach the website's hosting company in two possible scenarios: if the bully actually owns the domain, or if the people who run the website have been unresponsive or unhelpful.

In those cases, you'll need to find out who "hosts" the website. That's the company the website owner pays to actually put the website on the Internet. Some of the very large websites are their own hosts, but smaller and medium-size sites generally have third-party hosting companies, and those companies can pull the website down if the website owner isn't complying with the terms of their agreement with the host. Often, the agreement with the host includes a clause specifying that there will be no defamatory material on the website.

To figure out who hosts the site, visit any of these:

- www.arin.net/whois

- www.whois.net

- www.internic.net/whois.html

- www.betterwhois.com

Type in the domain name, and it'll show you details of who registered the domain name, who the administrative contact is, and the domain servers. The domain servers are important: they usually show you the website address of the hosting company. Using my site as an example again, you'll find this listed as my name servers:

ns1.gapc.net

ns2.gapc.net

Ignore whatever comes before the first period, and substitute in "www." So in this case, my hosting company is www.gapc.net. If the harassment was on my website, and I had ignored your messages, you'd visit them to lodge a complaint. You'd send the same kind of letter you had sent to me, but this time, you'd add in "Your client has ignored the e-mails I've sent on [date] and [date]." If you can point out where the postings violate the AUP or TOS, all the better. Quote the passage(s).

Notify the School

If the bully or bullies go to school with your child, notify the principal about what's going on. Principals' responsibilities in cyberbullying incidents are not always clear; their jurisdiction doesn't extend to situations that happen off school grounds. However, if the cyberbullying also happens at school, or if it affects the environment at school, they may be able to (and required to) intervene. It is important to notify the school especially if any of the kids involved may be at school, because cyberbullying may indicate other bullying problems with these same kids.

Schools should have filters in place to prevent kids from accessing sites where they're likely to get involved with bullying. Many schools block social networking sites, and disallow instant messaging on school computers. However, at this point, most don't block cell phones—which means students can still text-message each other, and can e-mail each other from school grounds.

I believe that school officials should get involved with cyberbullying incidents, whether the actual offenses happen on or off school grounds, because they inevitably affect the target's ability to function in school. However, many want to tackle only what happens at the school, and laws can actually discourage them from getting involved in events that occur outside of school.

Even if they don't take any disciplinary actions, however, they can be on the alert to watch your child more closely at school, and can address cyberbullying in classroom discussions.

In summer camps, we have been working to create policies for camp owners to prevent kids from cyberbullying between the seasons, when kids try to maintain their connections. Ask your child if any camp friends or counselors have posted or said anything negative about her online. Ask her if she knows of any postings on MySpace.com from counselors or campers and if any of these postings have been negative. Watch your child's reaction to see if this has occurred, and if so, make a plan to contact the camp owner and discuss any objective evidence you have printed or saved, if it is available. Camp owners are more interested in this than ever before, so include them in your discussions if it involves other kids or counselors.

Volunteers Who Help Track Cyberbullies

If you need help identifying a cyberbully or figuring out what to do next, there are several organizations ready to help.

- **www.haltabusektd.org.** This is the group Working to Halt Online Abuse, Kids/Teen Division. They say, "Our volunteers are specially trained to work with kids and teens currently experiencing online bullying, harassment or stalking, and to help others learn how to avoid such harassment or minimize its impact if it does occur."

- **www.cyberangels.org.** Founded by Guardian Angels leader Curtis Sliwa, this group consists of thousands of volunteers who can work with you to track down stalkers and bullies online.

- **www.wiredsafety.com.** This group has a "Cyber911 Tipline" where you can send reports about cyberabuse, such as cyberstalking, identity theft, and child exploitation. If the situation

LEARN TEXT ABBREVIATIONS

 Teens and preteens have a language all their own when it comes to e-mail, text messaging, and chats. Here are some of the common abbreviations they use:

401: I don't know	FYEO: For your eyes only
A3: Anywhere, anyplace, anytime	FYI: For your information
AFK: Away from computer	GF: Girlfriend
A/S/L: Age, sex, location?	IMHO: In my humble opinion
BBL: Be back later	IMO: In my opinion
BF: Boyfriend (or best friend)	IRL: In real life
BGWM: Be gentle with me	JK: Just kidding
BRB: Be right back	LMAO: Laughing my *ss off
BTW: By the way	LOL: Laughing out loud
DIKU: Do I know you?	MorF: Male or female?
F2F: Face to face	MOS: Mother over shoulder
F2T: Free to talk	OIC: Oh, I see
FOS: Father over shoulder	OMG: Oh my God
FWIW: For what it's worth	PCM: Please call me

involves any sort of offline risk (e.g., if the bullying involves death threats), you must first report it to your local police before Wired Safety will get involved.

- **www.ncvc.org.** If you're more comfortable on the phone, the National Crime Victims Center has a toll-free hotline you can use to ask for help. Call 1-800-FYI-CALL.

PM: Private message	TY: Thank you
POS: Parents over shoulder	TYVM: Thank you very much
PRW: Parents are watching	W2G (or WTG): Way to go
RL: Real life	WAYF: Where are you from?
ROFL: Rolling on the floor laughing	W/B: Write back
SOMY: Sick of me yet?	WB: Welcome back
TPTB: The powers that be	WTF. What the f^^^?
TTYL: Talk to you later	

These abbreviations are the language your children may be learning and using, so if you happen to walk in their room during instant messaging and see "POS," you've probably just learned that your child stopped communicating with her buddy online. If she doesn't come clean with you as to what she was talking about, then you need to put up your own radar.

Here are other resources to find out the meanings of acronyms used online:

- www.netlingo.com/emailsh.cfm

- www.webopedia.com/quick_ref/textmessageabbreviations.asp

- www.mistupid.com/internet/chattalk.htm

Happy Slapping

Around 2004 in London, a disturbing new trend caught the media's attention. It's called "happy slapping." One or more kids attack someone and capture a video of the incident, usually on a cell phone's recording device.

In its "purest" form, the idea is for a teenager to walk up to an unsuspecting person and slap him or her in the face (but not hard enough to bruise or do any real damage), while the teen's friends capture the target's surprised reaction on video. Then the kids can pass the videos around from cell phone to cell phone, or upload it to the Internet.

But it's really become a misnomer, because the attacks have often gone way beyond a simple "slap," and there's nothing "happy" about them, except for the perverse pleasure some bullies get out of random violence and humiliating a target. Sometimes it's done in gangs, and the targets can be anyone from a stranger in a subway to a classmate in the lunchroom.

Sixteen-year-old Becky Smith was the target of one of these attacks. She was attacked near her home, knocked out, and temporarily paralyzed. A girl beat her up while about five boys watched and videotaped, then they showed the video around school while Becky was in the hospital. Even her younger brother saw the video, and the girl was scared and humiliated about returning to school. The girl who attacked her was arrested, but not charged—she was let off with a warning, to the horror of Becky and her mom. The school did not discipline any of the students involved, saying on record that it was a police matter that happened off school grounds.

Groups of teens have even filmed themselves committing random murder. A fourteen-year-old girl went up to a thirty-seven-year-old man and told him they were making a documentary on happy slapping and told him to smile for the camera, according to court testimony . . . then she and three boys kicked and punched the man to death. The group of kids admitted that they had carried out about twenty other "happy slapping" incidents before this one, and they were all found guilty of manslaughter.

The term "happy slapping" hasn't caught on in the United States, but that doesn't mean the same types of events don't happen here. Bullies love having an audience, and mobile phone technology and similar small cameras make it possible for them to show off their abuse effortlessly even to people who were nowhere near the scene of the crime.

A thirteen-year-old from Long Island, New York, got into an online argument with three teenage girls over a boy, and they met her at an elementary school and savagely beat her up . . . while a friend of theirs taped it. They then put the video on websites such as YouTube and Photobucket, where it was downloaded thousands of times. The three bullies were arrested and charged with juvenile delinquency and attempted assault.

Some people think kids are getting ideas from shows like *Jackass* that blur the line between harmless pranks and criminal behavior, and that the bullies want some of that kind of attention. Some of them want to watch it by themselves or with friends later and laugh; others crave a bigger stage to show off their bullying power. The clear intent is to scare and humiliate a target.

Because of these kinds of problems, many schools have banned the use of cell phones altogether. Parents generally complain about that action because they want their kids to be able to call home when needed, or to have a way to reach out in case of emergency. But it's becoming increasingly clear that many students are not using their phones for worthy causes, so compromises need to be made. Some schools now collect cell phones at the start of each day and give them back at the end of the day; others bar individual students from using cell phones only after they've been caught with offensive material.

If you find out that your child is being harassed by phone, inform your phone service provider. Most calls can be traced, and they may be able to block the calls or to let you know where they're coming from so you can report abuses.

I urge you to check your children's camera phones for offensive videos and pictures of bullying incidents. Kids who've been involved with attacks should not be allowed to own mobile phones with built-in cameras. Even with Google's purchase of YouTube, I think it's a good idea to check with your kids and ask what they have downloaded from there. Your kids will at first be excited to see that you know something about this, but it will give you information on the kinds of things your kids are interested in and want to have on their own computers.

It's a Cyberworld

Sometimes it can seem tempting just to keep kids away from computers altogether! We hear stories about kids being stalked by predators, and threatened by bullies, and it all sounds pretty awful. But the truth is that computers and the Internet are far too helpful for kids to try to cut off the technology altogether. The reality is, the Internet is here to stay and has replaced the phone calls of a generation ago as a new social life.

Kids who are shy or bullied in person may find social groups online where they feel that they fit in. They may use e-mail to keep in touch with friends from old schools or camp. They may use the Internet as both a learning tool and a social tool, and just as in other areas of life, they may test out their boundaries in this medium and need to have an enforced set of guidelines.

Chances are good that your child understands the "cyberculture" better than you do. They're the ones who've literally grown up with computers and the Internet. But don't let a lack of understanding turn to panic—talk to your child about what he does online, and where he hangs out. If there's a problem, rest assured that you can handle it. Keep checking the sites we gave you and my own, www.respectu.com, for the newest information on bullying.

EIGHT

Special Needs and Disability Harassment

Kids with special needs—such as Asperger syndrome and other autistic spectrum disorders, learning disabilities, physical disabilities, developmental delays—are particularly vulnerable to bullying. They're seen as easy targets, and they're often less socially skilled than their peers, which can mean that they have extreme reactions to bullying. One of the problems is that, because of their reactions (often aggressive), teachers and other authority figures may get it wrong and think it's the target who is to blame. The more socially skilled bully can pretend he wasn't doing anything wrong, or was just joking around, when this other child just snapped! Thus, kids with special needs frequently get punished not because they actually caused the problem, but because they didn't know how to get the harassment to stop in an appropriate way. In other words, they get set up.

Generally, kids who have an actual diagnosis and are in special classes with aides have a better chance of being shielded from bullies. Adults know to look out for them, and they generally have peer groups who they can mingle with. The ones who may have it worst are the kids who don't have a diagnosis and don't have any special resources, but are at the bottom of their classes.

It's more effective for schools to put their limited resources to use watching over the "bottom 20 percent" of kids on the social ladder, rather than trying to watch the 80 percent who are rarely picked on. School personnel need to be made aware of which kids are targets, so people can watch out for them in school hotspots such as the cafeteria and the playground.

Qualities That Make Kids with Special Needs Easy Targets

Aside from the fact that they may look different and speak different from other kids, there are certain factors that are common among kids with special needs, and can cause them to be easier bullying targets.

- **Not good at understanding sarcasm and teasing.** Often, a vicious kid will pretend to be a child's friend, when he's actually making fun of him for the amusement of friends. His tone and his words may not match, and your special-needs child might not understand what's going on—at least until the bully does something truly mean. It's important for parents and teachers to define bullying for children who may not recognize it, and give plenty of examples of what bullying "looks" like and "sounds" like.

- **Outdated fashion.** Many kids with special needs don't follow fashion and hair trends like other kids—thus, they rely on their parents' sense of style, which doesn't often fly with their peers.

This is a correctable problem. Try to pay attention to current styles if you don't want your child to have an additional social handicap.

- **Aggressive or inappropriate responses.** Kids with special needs are often bad at tempering their responses when they're upset. They may react with extreme anger, tears, pulling on their hair, throwing a fit, etc.—all of which bullies love.

- **Easy to persuade.** Kids with special needs are often eager to please and want to fit in, so they'll do what other kids tell them to do, even if it's degrading or will get them in trouble.

- **Hygiene problems.** Kids with special needs are often not as conscious of cleanliness as other kids, and may have messy eating habits, forget to wear deodorant, and so on. Don't let this be the reason other kids pick on her: Even if you don't see the big deal if she wants to skip a shower or eat with her hands, other kids do. It's important that you enforce strict hygiene rules and manners—for your child's sake.

- **Inappropriate affection.** One mother was heartbroken that she had to be called in to the principal's office to discuss the fact that her son was hugging and kissing people. Surely, it was the other kids who should be taught that affection is good, she thought—but the other kids were using it as a reason to make cracks about his sexuality, call him a "retard," and generally shun him. It was also making teachers and bus drivers uncomfortable. His parents had to set out strong guidelines about where and when affection was appropriate.

- **Few friends.** Often, kids with special needs don't have many friends—and that's an important predictor that they'll be easy targets for bullies. They lack the buffers they need. If they do have friends, these friends are probably on the bottom of the

CHEYENNE'S STORY

Because of her hearing impairments, Cheyenne began wearing hearing aids to school, but found out that they had an unwanted side effect. Now that her hearing was better, she could hear kids whispering behind her. They'd whisper her name, and when she turned around, they'd pretend no one had said anything, or stare at her and sarcastically ask, "What?"

She was bullied badly through middle school and most of high school, and didn't have any friends. "If I were nominated for anything—say, Winter Dance Queen or Homecoming Queen—it was so they could project me up so that they could make fun of me even more. Finally, I convinced my parents to forget the hearing aid; it only seemed to make things worse."

She got blamed for things she didn't do, and was even thrown out of her own senior prom by a classmate. Several of her peers told her privately, "That wasn't right," or other expressions of sympathy, but no one spoke up for her. "I know that even if one person would have stood up, I would have been very grateful for their efforts to stand up for what they believed was right. And it would have given my self-esteem a boost."

social totem pole with them, and may not know how to react to help them in case of a bullying incident.

Character Education

These days, many teachers try to mix character education in with the more traditional academics. Most teachers do have lessons about diversity and acceptance of others. It's important to start teaching kids at a very early age that differences are okay, and that "different" doesn't mean "bad." Here, the teaching of empathy and acceptance of differences goes hand in hand to prevent bullying.

Although she remembers too many days when she came home from school and cried her heart out, the bullying subsided at the end of high school. "During this hard time, I discovered writing and realized I was pretty good at writing out my feelings and describing things on paper," she says. An English teacher encouraged her, and writing became her refuge. That's what she's doing now: working on becoming a full-time writer.

Her torment ended about five years ago; she's now a twenty-three-year-old single mom, but every day, she still feels the effects of being bullied. "It is never a good thing having to enter the real world with a really bad self-image, because more times than not, the image you see of yourself is the image you also project of yourself to others. It's not so easy to just wake up one day and feel peppy and self-confident. I truly believe that it takes only minutes to strip away a person's confidence—but it takes years to build it back up. Some people are extremely resilient; others are not. But I find that the people who were kicked around in their school years are also some of the nicest people you'll ever meet. They know how it feels to be treated badly and they don't want to inflict that pain on others."

If the teacher is not particularly adept at addressing these subjects, there are many resources designed to help. All students need to be taught what disabilities are, and how to treat people with special needs. Some of the tools a teacher may use:

- **Kids on the Block.** This educational puppet troupe has skits about various disabilities and medical issues, as well as programs about bullying and school safety. There are many troupes across the United States and abroad, and they are typically hired to perform in schools. Visit www.kotb.com or call 1-800-368-KIDS to find out if there's one in your area.

- **Picture books.** There are many children's books on topics related to special needs. "Special Needs in School" is one such series, published by JayJo Books (www.jayjo.com), and it includes titles about autism, asthma, diabetes, cerebral palsy, Down syndrome, dyslexia, Tourette's syndrome, and others. Teachers can read and discuss these books in class.

- **Guest speakers.** The school can ask guest speakers to talk about the impact disabilities have had on their lives.

- **Videos.** Some production companies exist solely to produce videos about disabilities for the educational market. Coulter Video (www.coultervideo.com) is one of these companies— begun by parents of a child with Asperger syndrome, they produce videos about Asperger syndrome and autism, meant to be shown in classrooms. They say, "One mother of a son with Asperger syndrome said that after a school assembly in which the video was played by a psychologist, classmates apologized to her son for the way they'd treated him, began sitting with him at lunch and included him in sports—in spite of his lack of physical skills."

Bullying Within Special Education Classes

It's not always a matter of nondisabled students picking on kids with disabilities. The real bullying may occur *between* kids with special needs. Many times, there are teachers or other adults around to protect kids with special needs when they interact with other students. However, the socialization that goes on within the special needs group is where the learning needs to occur.

When kids with special needs can learn social tools to recognize when someone is getting angry or upset when they themselves are pushing buttons, it sets up a safer environment for these behaviors to be tested in the broader population. Adults need to role-play and practice these skills with the kids and give them opportunities to practice them within their group before venturing out. The more kids with disabilities can test out these skills with adults or peer models nearby, in actual situations to coach them, the better chance there is for them to learn.

The Laws of Disability Harassment

The Office for Civil Rights (OCR) and the Office of Special Education and Rehabilitative Services (OSERS) within the United States Department of Education sent out a letter to school principals, superintendents, and college and university presidents in 2000 reminding them that disability harassment was a very important issue, and that the problem seemed to be growing: they were fielding phone calls and witnessing court cases on this topic at an alarming rate. Therefore, they wrote a letter that included the following:

> Schools, colleges, universities, and other educational institutions have a responsibility to ensure equal educational opportunities for all students, including students with disabilities. This responsibility is based on Section 504 of the Rehabilitation Act of 1973 (Section 504) and Title II of the Americans with Disabilities Act of 1990 (Title II), which are enforced by OCR. Section 504 covers all schools, school districts, and colleges and universities receiving federal funds. Title II covers all state and local entities, including school districts and public institutions of higher education, whether or not they receive federal funds. Disability harassment is a form of discrimination

prohibited by Section 504 and Title II. Both Section 504 and Title II provide parents and students with grievance procedures and due process remedies at the local level. Individuals and organizations also may file complaints with OCR.

The letter sought to remind educators that states and schools were responsible to ensure a free appropriate public education to eligible students with disabilities, and that parents could file complaints with the Office of Civil Rights or their state educational agency if they felt their children's education was being denied because of disability harassment. They concluded:

> Schools, school districts, colleges, and universities have a legal responsibility to prevent and respond to disability harassment. As a fundamental step, educational institutions must develop and disseminate an official policy statement prohibiting discrimination based on disability and must establish grievance procedures that can be used to address disability harassment. A clear policy serves a preventive purpose by notifying students and staff that disability harassment is unacceptable, violates federal law, and will result in disciplinary action. The responsibility to respond to disability harassment, when it does occur, includes taking prompt and effective action to end the harassment and prevent it from recurring and, where appropriate, remedying the effects on the student who was harassed.

Their recommendations for schools included a written policy prohibiting discrimination based on disability, discussion of disabilities in the classroom, encouraging reporting of bullying incidents, counseling for both targets and bullies, monitoring programs to follow up after bullying incidents, and appropriate training for staff and students to recognize disability harassment.

PARENTS' ROLES IN SPECIAL-NEEDS BULLYING

Parents play such an important role in this area. Children learn how to react to kids with special needs based largely on how their parents react to people who are "different" or "outside the norm." Pay close attention to your body language and verbal cues when you see someone walking with a brace in the mall, or see someone with a physical abnormality. If you stare, roll your eyes, or make disapproving comments, your child is going to be much more likely to think it's okay to pick on kids with special needs.

You can call the Office of Civil Rights or the Office of Special Education and Rehabilitative Services at 1-800-USA-LEARN to learn more.

Talking to Your Kids About People with Special Needs

It's understandable for children to feel uncomfortable or even scared when they're faced with someone who looks or acts different from what they'd expect. This can lead to some pretty embarrassing moments when your child points and asks too loudly, "What's wrong with him, Mommy?" (If it helps, know that most parents of kids with special needs who I've known fully understand that young kids don't mean harm when they do things like this.)

Continually teach your child that "different" doesn't mean "bad." One of the best things you can do is to convey how cool it is for people to overcome their challenges and obstacles. Try to avoid sending your child too many messages that you feel *bad* for people with special needs, or that they need sympathy. This encourages the mentality that they're inferior because of their disabilities.

You can explain any clear issues you spot—"His legs don't work like yours, so he uses that chair on wheels to get around instead of walking." Or "She uses that stick because she can't see . . . It helps her to feel what's in front of her so she doesn't bump into things."

Intellectual and emotional disabilities are sometimes trickier to explain, but if you keep the concepts simple, you can be honest without being insulting. When describing someone with mental challenges, you can say, "He doesn't learn as fast as you do. He has to work harder to learn things that are easy for you, like [fill in examples]." When describing someone with autism or similar disorders, you can say, "His brain works a little different from yours, so it's harder for him to communicate with people like you do."

Some important points to make when easing your child's concerns are:

- You can't catch it. It's not contagious like a cold is.

- It isn't anyone's fault. He didn't do something wrong.

- It's something she was born with, and she'll always have it.

- There's a lot she can do anyway, and lots of things she can be good at.

A Positive Spin on Challenges

Kids with special needs can be an inspiration for kids without disabilities. "What a challenge that boy faces," you might say. "And look at how well he's doing. Why do you think he's smiling? What's he happy about? How do you think you would handle it if you had to wear leg braces and a helmet like that? What do you have to deal with that's a real challenge for you?"

You might try brainstorming with your child about what the other person's life is like. What things would be different, and what would be the same? The other person might need a lift to get up stairs, or might not be able to ride a bike or recite the ABCs. But maybe they like the same TV shows or music, and love pizza, and both have dogs. If you can help your child see some potential common ground, it can be easier for him to have empathy.

A friend of mine has two sons, seven and ten, who are particularly wonderful to kids with disabilities. It seems that they manage to find and befriend every kid who has a physical or mental disability. They'll go skate with a boy at the roller rink who's slower than everyone else, or sit next to the boy in church who's an amputee and strike up a conversation. When I asked her what she taught them that enables them to be so comfortable around kids with special needs, she said, "I just tell them how I think it's so cool that kids can be so strong. We talk about how you have to be a really special person to face tough challenges like that. We don't talk about what people can't do—we talk about what they *can* do that's surprising."

To encourage this, they read books and watch movies about people with challenges, and talk about them afterward. For example, they'll read about an artist who paints with the brush in her mouth instead of her hands because she has cerebral palsy, or watch a movie about a challenged athlete, and afterward, they talk about kids they know who could grow up and do things just like that.

When you talk to your kids about people with disabilities, don't forget some of the more common problems, like stuttering, which affects about 5 percent of preschoolers and 1 percent of adults. Teach your kids that kids who stutter know what they want to say; they just have a little trouble getting the words to come out, and no one should tease them for that.

Backlash from Mainstreaming

Another recent problem is that not all parents are happy that kids with special needs are included in "regular" classes. There has been much evidence to show that kids with special needs learn more when they're mainstreamed as much as possible, rather than segregated into special schools and separate classrooms all the time. However, this sometimes causes parents of nondisabled kids to complain that their kids are being "dragged behind" or are not getting enough attention because the kids with special needs are using up too much of the teachers' attention.

This usually comes from parents who are ultracompetitive. Sometimes, those parents will even push for their own kids to be diagnosed with *something* so they can get the "competitive edge" of having an aide assigned to them, or extra time to take tests, or additional tutoring. In essence, they play the system, figuring they'll take advantage of whatever they can for their kids to get the most attention.

It's not a healthy mind-set, nor does it set a good example for the kids. It teaches kids that parents have no respect for kids with disabilities, so why should they? Those parents see these kids as a nuisance and dead weight, so why would their kids think any differently?

But diversity benefits everyone, and parents who spend their days looking for ways to exclude others, get special attention, and cheat the school system are hurting everyone in the class.

Special Instructions for Special Needs

If your child is being bullied at school because of a disability, in addition to the steps and suggestions I've outlined in the previous chapters (documenting all incidents, talking to teachers, and so on), ask for a meeting with the Individualized Education Program (IEP) team, or the Section 504 team (named after Section 504 of the Rehabilitation Act of 1973), which are there to ensure that the school district is properly meeting the needs of students with disabilities.

They can be your advocates, and help to ensure that a plan is enacted to keep your child safe from bullies. They can also make sure the problem is addressed on a wider level, such as including more disability-related material in the classroom. You can also ask for special counseling for your child if the bullying has affected him badly, or for a peer leader or peer tutor to "buddy up" with your child.

AFTERWORD

As scary and infuriating as bullying incidents are, they can also be the catalysts for great personal growth. They can help your children learn true self-esteem and make them realize that they have power to stand tall even when others try to make them feel small. And when you, as a parent, help your child through traumatic events, your relationship can grow even closer. Your child learns that you're someone he can count on.

Some problems will be solved relatively simply. Just learning the right comeback lines or how not to react or separating the bully from the target may end the problem. Other problems will be more complex, and may require a multipronged approach over several months or even years. But whatever it takes, and however long it takes, trust that both you and your child will get through it if you continue working on it together.

The fact that you are aware of the problem and are concerned enough to take steps to learn how to help your child means that your child already has an important advantage: a caring parent who now has an array of knowledge on this topic, and skills to teach to help the child become a less attractive target.

I hope you feel confident with your new tools; you're now more educated about bullying than most of the public. As you put these tools to use, however, keep in mind that it's like following a dinner recipe. You can always personalize the instructions, add your own ingredients, fit the tastes of your family. If you try the dish one way and find that it's not quite right for you, don't be afraid to rewrite the recipe a bit and try again.

If I can be of further assistance to you, my cyberdoor is always open. You can visit me online at www.respectu.com, where I offer a free newsletter and information about my telephone coaching services and programs for schools and camps.

In addition, the "Questions and Answers" section on my website and in my newsletter offers readers of this book a chance to communicate their challenges and concerns. Although I'm not able to personally answer every question I receive, I will regularly post my responses to select reader questions, so please feel free to drop me a line.

I wish you great success in keeping your children bullyproof for life.

RESOURCES

BULLIES 2 BUDDIES
Phone: (718) 983-1333
www.bullies2buddies.com
A website that includes an excellent, humorous, free manual for kids who are being bullied, to enforce the idea of not reacting emotionally to bullies.

BULLY POLICE
Phone: (509) 547-1052
www.bullypolice.org
Founded by a mother whose son killed himself because of bullying, this is a watchdog organization that campaigns for better bullying laws and advocates for bullied children.

CYBERANGELS
www.cyberangels.org
Thousands of volunteers who can work with you to track down stalkers and bullies online.

FIGHT CRIME: INVEST IN KIDS
1212 New York Ave. NW, Suite 300
Washington, DC 20005
Phone: (202) 776-0027
A "national, bipartisan, nonprofit anti-crime organization of more than 3,000 police chiefs, sheriffs, prosecutors, other law enforcement

leaders and violence survivors . . . Our organization focuses on high quality early education programs, prevention of child abuse and neglect, after-school programs for children and teens, and interventions to get troubled kids back on track."

KIDS AGAINST BULLYING
PACER Center
Bullying Prevention Project
8161 Normandale Boulevard
Minneapolis, MN 55437
Phone: (952) 838-9000
www.pacerkidsagainstbullying.org
A website for kids about bullying. Games, contests, writing by kids, videos, an advice column, and more.

KIDS ON THE BLOCK
9385-C Gerwig Lane
Columbia, MD 21046
Phone: (800) 368-KIDS
www.kotb.com
Puppet troupes that visit schools to address issues about disabilities and bullying.

MIX IT UP
www.mixitup.org
A program to encourage kids to break up cliques and socialize with new people at school.

NATIONAL CRIME VICTIMS CENTER
Phone: (800) FYI-CALL
www.ncvc.org
A toll-free hotline you can use to ask for help with bullying situations.

National Youth Violence Prevention
Resource Center
P.O. Box 10809
Rockville, MD 20849-0809
Phone: (866) SAFEYOUTH (866-723-3968) 8 a.m. to 6 p.m. ET
Monday to Friday
www.safeyouth.org/scripts/teens/bullying.asp
Offers free access to hundreds of brochures, fact sheets, reports, posters, and other print publications about youth violence prevention. Has a special section about bullying and a toll-free hotline.

Office of Civil Rights
U.S. Department of Education
Customer Service Team
550 12th Street, SW
Washington, DC 20202-1100
Phone: (800) USA-LEARN
www.ed.gov/about/offices/list/ocr
"We serve student populations facing discrimination and the advocates and institutions promoting systemic solutions to civil rights problems. An important responsibility is resolving complaints of discrimination."

RespectU
(914) 428-0004 ex. 23
www.respectu.com
A resource for parents about all sorts of bullying: school, camp, sports, cyberbullying, and corporate.

THE SAFETYZONE
NWREL
101 SW Main Street, Suite 500
Portland, OR 97204
www.safetyzone.org
Offers free school safety technical assistance guides for download.

SCHOOL COP
www.schoolcopsoftware.com
Free software to help school staff map where bullying incidents occur
around school.

STOP BULLYING NOW
http://stopbullyingnow.hrsa.gov
For kids and adults. Offers tips, an advice column, animated
"webisodes" about bullying, and ways to help.

WIRED SAFETY
www.wiredsafety.com
This group has a "Cyber911 Tipline" where you can send reports
about cyberabuse, such as cyberstalking, identity theft, and child
exploitation. If the situation involves any sort of offline risk (e.g., if the
bullying involves death threats), you must first report it to your local
police before Wired Safety will get involved.

WORKING TO HALT ONLINE ABUSE:
KIDS-TEEN DIVISION
www.haltabusektd.org
"Our volunteers are specially trained to work with kids and teens currently experiencing online bullying, harassment or stalking, and to
help others learn how to avoid such harassment or minimize its impact
if it does occur."

NOTES

1. Nansel, T. R. et al. "Bullying behaviors among U.S. youth: Prevalence and association with psychosocial adjustment." *Journal of the American Medical Association* 285 (16): 2094–100, 2001.
2. McCabe, R. E. et al. "Preliminary examination of the relationship between anxiety disorders in adults and self-reported history of teasing or bullying experiences." *Cognitive Behaviour Therapy* 32 (4): 187-93, November 2003.
3. Fekkes, M. et al. "Bullying behavior and associations with psychosomatic complaints and depression in victims." *The Journal of Pediatrics* 144 (1): 17–22, January 2004.
4. Baldry, A. C. "Bullying in schools and exposure to domestic violence." *Child Abuse & Neglect* 27 (7): 713–32, July 2003.
5. Sheard, C. et al. "Bullying and people with severe intellectual disability." *Journal of Intellectual Disability Research* 45 (Pt 5): 407–15, October 2001.
6. Shields, A., Cicchetti, D. "Parental maltreatment and emotion dysregulation as risk factors for bullying and victimization in middle childhood." *Journal of Clinical Child Psychology* 30 (3): 349–63, September 2001.
7. Schoenberg, J. et al. "Feeling safe: What girls say." Executive Summary. Girl Scouts Research Institute, 2003.
8. Baldry, A. C. "'What about bullying?' An experimental field study to understand students' attitudes towards bullying and victimization in Italian middle schools." *The British Journal of Educational Psychology* 74 (Pt. 4): 583–98, December 2004.
9. Rusby, J. C. et al. "Relationships between peer harassment and adolescent problem behaviors." *The Journal of Early Adolescence* 25 (4): 453–77, 2005.
10. "Long-term effects of bullying." *Kidscape*, November 1999.
11. Vossekuil, B. et al. "The final report and findings of the Safe School Initiative: Implications for the prevention of school attacks in the United States." U.S. Secret Service and U.S. Department of Education, May 2002.
12. "Man blows self up in botched attack on old high school bully." *Mainichi*. Japan, July 13, 2003.

13. "Sticks, stones and bullies." CBC News Online, March 23, 2005.
14. Castrucci, B. C., Gerlach, K. K. "Understanding the association between authoritative parenting and adolescent smoking." *Maternal and Child Health Journal*, March 23, 2006.
15. DeVore, E. R., Ginsburg, K. R. "The protective effects of good parenting on adolescents." *Current Opinion in Pediatrics* 17 (4): 460–65, August 2005.
16. Baumrind, D. "The influence of parenting style on adolescent competence and substance use." *Journal of Early Adolescence* 11 (1): 56–95, 1991.
17. Koestner, R., Franz, C., Weinberger, J. "The family origins of empathic concern: a 26-year longitudinal study." *Journal of Personality and Social Psychology* 58 (4): 709-17, April 1990.
18. "Bullied: Silent tears." I-Team 8 Investigative Report. WISH-TV, Indianapolis, November 2002 and September 2003.
19. Bixler, M. "Teen accused of bus-stop murder released on bond." *Atlanta Journal-Constitution*, December 4, 1998.
20. "Get to big answers on bullying." *The Enquirer*, Cincinnati, April 27, 2006.
21. "Kansas teen awarded $250K in bullying lawsuit." NBC San Diego, August 12, 2005.
22. "Conn. bullying lawsuit settled," Associated Press, August 23, 2005.
23. Brittain, C. "Boy says coach paid him $25 to injure player," *Pittsburgh Tribune-Review*, July 16, 2005.
24. Liu, C. "Boy, 13, gets 12 years for murder." *Los Angeles Times*, July 29, 2005.
25. Ybarra, M. L. et al. "Examining characteristics and associated distress related to Internet harassment: Findings from the Second Youth Internet Safety Survey." *Pediatrics* 118 (4): e1169–77, October 2006.
26. Struglinski, S. "Schoolyard bullying has gone high tech." *Deseret News*, August 18, 2006.

INDEX

Q

questionnaire for parents, 82–85
  for self-awareness, 88
  for self-evaluation, 85–88

R

Recognize, Act, and Preserve (RAP)
  acting on a plan, 59–69 (*see also*
    bully stopper guide)
  preserve, 69–78 (*see also*
    friendships, working on;
    social confidence, gaining)
  recognizing the problem, 37–59
    (*see also* speaking to children
    about bullying, how to)
Redmond, Poppy, 180–81
Rehabilitation Act of 1973, 261
relational bullying, 24–25
  dealing with, 68–69
restitutions, brainstorming, 54
role-playing, 45, 64–66
Rolfe, Tracey, 124–26
romantic relationships, 31
Rusby, Julie, 31

S

"safety people," 117
"safety zones," 117–18
school, bullying in, 31, 113–59,
    156–57
  "community building days,"
    encouraging, 147–48
  group bullying, 148
  "hot spots," identifying, 135
  lawyer involvement, 156–57
  "lunch bunches," 149
  moving to a new school/changing
    classes, 149–53
    parent checklist for schools,
    151–52

parental involvement, stepping in,
    124–26
parent/teacher groups, banding
    together in, 154–56
peer leaders, 144–46
police involvement, 156
pulling child out of school, when
    to, 157–59
refusal to attend, resolving,
    114–18
resolving, child's involvement in,
    119–24
  comeback lines, 121–24
  Gail Lynch's story, 123
  Tracey Rolfe's story, 124–26
resolving, steps to take in, 118–19
  "safety people," 117
  "safety zones," 117–18, 137
shootings, 31–32, 188
system failure, tragic example of,
    153–54
teacher and principal involvement,
    126–44
see also antibullying policy,
    school; teacher and principal
    involvement
school avoidance, 44–45
"School Cop" program, 146
Schools Where Everyone Belongs
    (Davis), 217
self-defense classes, 73–74
self-esteem, 33, 34
self-esteem, 16
self-image, 99–100
sensitive children, 42, 52–54, 62,
    66–67, 129, 223
severe bullying, signs of, 115
sibling rivalry, 19–20
  birth order and, 20
Smith, Becky, 252

ABOUT THE AUTHORS

Joel Haber, Ph.D. (The Bully Coach), is a clinical psychologist who has devoted more than twenty years to the identification, prevention, and reduction of abusive behaviors in adults as well as children. He has studied the bully dynamic in many settings, including the home, schools, sports, and camps. He is the official bullying consultant for the American Camp Association.

Founder of the RespectU Program, Dr. Haber has held positions at the University of Alabama, Birmingham Medical School, White Plains Hospital, and New York Medical College, Department of Neurosurgery. He leads conference sessions and workshops for thousands of people annually on bullying and violence prevention.

A graduate of the State University of New York at Binghamton, Dr. Haber received his M.S. and Ph.D. from the University of Georgia in Clinical Psychology and Behavioral Medicine. His professional affiliations include the National Register of Psychology and the American Psychological Association. He is also a Diplomate Mental Health Service Provider in the field of sports psychology. His official website is www.respectu.com.

Jenna Glatzer is the author or ghostwriter of sixteen books. Among her latest are *Celine Dion: For Keeps* (Andrews McMeel, 2005) and *The Street-Smart Writer: Self-Defense Against Sharks and Scams in the Writing World* (Nomad Press, 2006). She's also a contributing editor at *Writer's Digest* and has written hundreds of magazine articles and essays for anthologies. She is the mother of a wonderful baby daughter. Her official website is www.jennaglatzer.com.

31901046673937